suddenly FRUGAL

HOW TO LIVE **HAPPIER & HEALTHIER** FOR LESS

LEAH INGRAM

Avon, Massachusetts

Published by
Adams Media, a division of F+W Media, Inc.
57 Littlefield Street, Avon, MA 02322. U.S.A.
www.adamsmedia.com

ISBN 10: 1-4405-0182-3
ISBN 13: 978-1-4405-0182-1

Printed in the United States of America.

10 9 8 7 6 5 4 3 2 1

Library of Congress Cataloging-in-Publication Data
is available from the publisher.

All savings listed herein are estimations and will vary depending on many factors including location, lifestyle, and the types of appliances/equipment you own. Before implementing any of the suggestions given in this book, please consult owner's manuals, instructions, and warranties for your particular items to ensure that no advice in this book would be contrary to the manufacturer's instruction. The author and publisher disclaim any liability of any kind arising directly or indirectly from the use of this book.

This book is available at quantity discounts for bulk purchases.
For information, please call 1-800-289-0963.

table of CONTENTS

acknowledgments

I'm a believer in karma and fate. And both had a big role in my taking the concept of living a suddenly frugal life from an idea to a blog to a book.

For starters, had I not been raised by a frugal mother, I never would have even considered dedicating my recent writing life to all things frugal. Of course, when I was growing up, I didn't know what to call my mother's shrewd habits—weird, perhaps? But as I grew older and wiser and recognized the wisdom in her money-saving ways, I came to appreciate the thriftiness she taught me. For that, thanks go out to my mother, Judy Watson Ingram, the original Yankee in my book.

Then there is the matter of my husband, Bill Behre, and me deciding to sell our old home and buy our new house some two years ago—a move that ended up not being financially prudent, but that helped us to fully embrace frugal living. Because we didn't want to end up as another foreclosure statistic, we knew we had to significantly change how we lived and spent money. My husband and my daughters, Jane and Annie, have been really good sports throughout this whole frugal experiment, and I thank them for their everlasting support of this and my many other professional endeavors.

Because we sold our house and bought a new one, we became even closer with our realtors and friends Michele Natale and Kim Sager at the Coldwell Banker Hearthside office in our town. Not only did these women listen to use as we blabbered on about our newly frugal ways, but they also introduced me to the local CSA farm of which I'm now a member. I'd also like to thank fellow realtor (and fellow author and frugalista) Dee Dee Bowman. She's schooled me on all things green and frugal, and

I value all of the advice and suggestions she's shared with me in the past few years. So thanks go out to Michele, Kim, and Dee Dee.

Now on to my agent Adam Chromy at Artists and Artisans. Though I've had a handful of agents with the thirteen other books I've written, Adam is the first agent who has been more than just the person who sells a book for me. Adam believes in me holistically, as a writer, an expert, and a brand. I have never had someone who wasn't related to me be such a cheerleader for my future success, and had Adam not believed in me so strongly, I know that *Suddenly Frugal* never would have happened. Plus, had I not filled in for my dear friend (now deceased) Sarah Wernick as a moderator at a writing conference a few years ago, I never would have met Adam, who was a speaker on the panel I was moderating. Thank you, Sarah and fate, for allowing Adam and me to meet. It took more than two years, Adam, but finally we've got a book in our hands, and greater things to come in the near future.

Were it not for Adam, I never would have been able to work with the fine folks at Adams Media again. (I wrote the second edition of *The Everything® Etiquette Book* for the company a few years back.) I'm thrilled to have the opportunity to work closely with editors Meredith O'Hayre and Laura Daly at Adams.

Finally, thank you to all of the loyal readers of my Suddenly Frugal blog: *www.suddenlyfrugal.com*. You all have shared great ideas with me, made awesome suggestions about topics I should cover in the future, and given me honest feedback when you felt my blog was slipping a bit off the frugal path. I hope you'll all stick around for many years to come, and tell everyone you know about my frugal mission.

introduction

THE MYTH OF FRUGALITY

I'm not shy about telling people why we decided to start living frugally back in 2007. We had gotten in over our heads with debt and then bought more house than we could afford. When I make this confession, most people reply, "Well, good for you for nipping the problem in the bud." I'm sure that behind our backs, they say, "Serves you right, you spendthrift, for buying a house you couldn't afford."

Some people actually called us freaks when we told them we had become a suddenly frugal family. They couldn't fathom that we could change how we live and what we spend in today's world, and how we could still come out ahead financially and socially, and actually be happy about it.

Now, granted, all of this name-calling occurred long before the economy sunk to the bottom of the toilet. It was still a time of freely available credit and conspicuous consumption. But more important, people didn't understand how or even *why* we would willingly become frugal. That's because these folks had bought into the myth of frugality. To them, living frugally meant not living much at all. But that's not the point of frugality—the "not living" part. In reality, if you adopt a more frugal lifestyle, suddenly you will find that you are more in control of your spending and you will actually be able to live more on less.

It's like the people I met long ago when I joined Weight Watchers, who believed that if they ate too little each day, they would lose more weight. These people had determined from day one on Weight Watchers that they would undercut their Points intake every day so they could get skinnier faster.

While that theory sounds perfect, it is flawed. Your body needs a certain amount of calories each day to function, and if you shortchange your body, it will fight your attempt to lose weight. Once you start tracking how many Points you could and should eat each day, you'll discover that you can eat more food than you initially thought, and you can enjoy your mealtimes more.

It's no different with living frugally. You will still be able to spend money—you'll just be spending it in new and different ways.

The Four Myths of Frugality

Obviously, you're interested in learning more about frugal living, or you wouldn't have picked up this book. But in case you have any lingering doubts about the terrible, horrible, no-good sacrifices you're going to have to make while living frugally, let me debunk the four myths of frugality.

Myth #1: Frugal people never have any fun.

Truth: Well, that depends on your definition of fun. If you enjoy paying a ridiculous cover charge at a dance club and drinking $100 bottles of champagne, well, then, yeah, you're not going to have much fun living frugally at home. However, if your idea of fun is more middle-of-the-road, I've got great news for you: even with cutting back on your expenses, you can still see first-run movies, read *New York Times* best-selling books, and stay abreast of the latest celebrity gossip with your favorite magazines. One way that you can do all of this? Your public library. (You do remember where the library is, right?) Or you can order movies On Demand through your cable company or Netflix (*www.netflix.com*), and spend $5 or less for a night at the movies for four instead of almost $40 or more at the theater. Or you can participate in something called PaperBackSwap (*www.paperbackswap.com*) so you can get your book fix for a lot less. Basically, even when you're living frugally, you can have your TiVo and watch it, too.

Myth #2: Living frugally means eating like a pauper.

Truth: When I first thought about living frugally, I thought my family would have to eat rice, beans, or pasta every night. I mean, think about the quintessential poor college student. What is she subsisting on? Ramen noodles, and rice and beans.

While ramen noodles and rice and beans can be a part of your frugal meal planning—if you happen to like them—I promise that you'll only have to use them in moderation, if at all. You can still serve your family chicken breasts and pork loin, fresh fruit and vegetables, and even dessert.

The trick to making this work on a frugal budget is getting into the habit of meal planning—and planning based on what's on sale at the supermarket, not what you feel like eating right then and there. That impulsive eating is what take-out is for—indulging your cravings—and trust me, you'll need to cut down on how frequently you order in if you want to save some dough.

Additionally, you'll want to take a long-term view toward stocking up on more expensive grocery items when they're on sale *and* you have a coupon. You may not actually need those lasagna noodles or chicken stock for this week's meal, but if they're priced right—and you know you could be cooking lasagna or a chicken dish in the near future—then you should buy them. This way, you have them when you do need them, and you bought them when they were dirt cheap! You'll be so proud of yourself when you're making that lasagna.

I know this approach to grocery shopping and meal planning probably sounds like common sense, but the truth is most people tell me, "Well, I don't have time to plan for meals or read the grocery flyer." You know what? I didn't think I had time to do that either, until I made time for it. It's just like exercise. I'll bet that if you've ever thought about losing weight, at first you probably thought you'd never find the time to exercise. But once you stopped the negative self-talk, you probably realized, "Well, if I park in the farthest spot at work and take the stairs instead of the elevator, I can easily get in fifteen or twenty minutes of exercise." And then once you started doing that, you probably said, "Now that wasn't that hard. I wonder what else I could do to sneak exercise into my day?"

Embracing frugal living works the same way. Once you decide to think about little changes you can make in how you buy your food, plan your meals, and cook your dinners, you're going to realize that (1) meal planning isn't as hard as it seems and (2) you can really save big bucks while serving your family great food.

Myth #3: If I'm frugal, I'll never get to shop again.

Truth: Well, you might have to give up "shopper-tainment," as we did—that was what we called it when we went shopping as entertainment, not when we actually needed to buy something. But I promise this: you won't have to avoid malls like the plague. You'll just have to put some thought into what you want to buy, and decide if you really need it, and if you will be able to get the best value possible for it.

Think about it this way: I don't want you to overspend on something that you didn't really need in the first place. At the same time, if you did really need that thing in the first place, I don't want you to *underspend* and buy a cheap, crappy version of the thing you wanted. You know that the cheap, crappy version is just going to break in two weeks anyway, and then you'll need to buy another—meaning you'll likely spend twice as much in the end. See where I'm going with this?

When you're frugal, you can still shop. But you're going to have to shop for the total value of something versus the short-term price. And you won't be alone: a recent *Brandweek* survey, conducted during the heart of the recession, showed that consumers are willing to shell out more money for a product (say, $150 for a pair of Nike sneakers) when they know they'll get value for their money. I'm the same way with an L.L. Bean down coat I bought for $200. I knew this coat would be well made and, should anything happen to it, L.L. Bean would stand behind its product 100 percent.

Sure, I cringed when I slapped down $200 for one stinking winter coat. But since L.L. Bean has a lifetime guarantee on its products, I knew that if that coat wore out, ripped, or got ruined, L.L. Bean would replace it for free. That basically meant that this $200 coat was the last winter jacket I would ever have to buy.

Myth #4: My kids are going to hate me if I ask them to be frugal.

Truth: Guess what? Your kids are probably going to complain no matter what you do. Even kids who are spoiled beyond belief whine about their parents. Besides, your job is to be your child's parent, not her best friend. So get over the fact that you might have to play the bad guy, and use your newfound frugality to teach your kids some valuable money lessons.

Here's one money lesson to start with: spending $50 on an Abercrombie T-shirt isn't a good deal, no matter how much you make or have in the bank. But you know what is a good deal? Explaining to your kids that with a little extra effort—visiting discount stores, checking consignment shops, or logging on to eBay—they can probably find that same shirt for a heck of a lot less than $50. Now that's a lifelong lesson your kids can take to the bank—quite literally, if you end up helping them to save money on their original purchase.

Make It a Family Affair

Now that we've debunked the myths of frugality, are you ready to start living more while spending less?

Perhaps the reason my family succeeded right out of the gate is because my husband and I both have frugality in our genes.

I grew up thinking it was normal that your drinking glasses used to be jelly jars, and that old Velveeta boxes had a second life as drawer organizers. And my husband's uncle used to give him and his cousins the "fun" job of hammering bent nails into straight nails so he could use them again. Okay, so this borders on *tightwad* more than *frugal,* but you get the idea.

How the Book Is Set Up

I'm confident that you'll find this book relevant for the long haul. Most experts agree that when the economy does bounce back, consumers will continue in their frugal ways. That's because the credit and equity free-for-all of the past decades won't be coming back anytime soon. Everyone is going to have to learn to live more on less—not for six months, but for the rest of their lives.

In this book, you'll find easy-to-understand advice, and some frugal highlights. For example, on my blog Suddenly Frugal (read and subscribe to it at *www.suddenlyfrugal.com*), I started something called the Suddenly Frugal Seal of Approval. I gave this so-called "seal" out to products and services from time to time when I felt that a particular product or service would help blog readers to better embrace frugal living. I've repeated some of those seal winners here in the book, and I've "given out" a few more of these seals to additional products; those awards are all unique to this book (look for the Seal of Approval logos).

In addition, so you can have a real sense of how much money you can save by adopting your suddenly frugal lifestyle, I end each chapter with a wrap-up called "Total Savings in This Chapter." That section is exactly what it sounds like—a dollar-and-cents survey of your potential savings, should you follow the suggestions in the preceding chapter. Your total may be lower or higher, of course, depending on where you live and your family's lifestyle.

While the blog gave birth to this book, it has continued to morph into its own virtual being. Keep in mind that, though this book will cover many of the same topics I've covered on the blog, *Suddenly Frugal*, the book, is not just a cut-and-paste of blog posts. The book is designed to be a thorough overview of how you can live frugally, and that's why I've expanded generously on many blog postings. Each chapter gives you more detailed information on what you need to know to live frugally—successfully and happily frugally, that is. Plus, this book can become a portable and convenient resource that you can take with you on the train to work, to your kids' sports practices, or wherever else you like to sneak in some useful reading.

You Can Do It!

To Bill and me, adopting frugal ways was like stepping into a pair of hand-me-down shoes. Even if frugality isn't in your DNA (thanks, Mom and Uncle Joe!), you really can learn to live more on less. The key to embracing frugal living is finding painless ways to make small changes in your daily habits. Trust me, these changes will end up saving you a bunch of money.

Many people I've talked to know one or two things they can do to cut back, such as minimizing vacations and meals out, but beyond that they're stumped. When they look at their current lifestyle, they have no idea where they can trim the fat without causing themselves social pain. That's exactly what this book will do. It will help you identify easy-to-adopt differences you can make in your day-to-day living that can add up to big savings—immediately! In many cases, you won't have to wait months or years to realize these savings. Plus, these changes will likely bring you closer together as a family and provide a stronger financial footing for the future.

Like those hand-me-down shoes, perhaps these changes won't be very comfortable at first. However, once you break them in, those habits will begin to feel like second nature. And I'll bet that once you realize how well you can live without spending a lot of money, you'll never go back to your spendthrift ways.

chapter one

REBOOTING YOUR DAILY ROUTINES

When you adopt a frugal lifestyle, start by re-examining your daily routines to make sure that you don't spend any more money than is necessary to get the job done—whatever that job may be. This chapter talks about tweaking such daily routines as cleaning, doing laundry, packing lunches, and cooking meals so you can get them done efficiently and inexpensively. In addition, with your daily routines come everyday expenses that might be up for reconsideration, now that you're looking to slice-and-dice your spending budget. This chapter gives you advice on how to do that, too.

Cleaning House

A few years ago I was a spokesperson for a certain cleaning product that was extremely convenient yet extremely pricey. Because I was going out on a ten-city media tour on behalf of this cleaning product, I had cases of it in my house. Even after the tour was over, I still had leftovers of this cleaning product, and I used it all the time to tidy up my house.

Then two things happened. One, I ran out of the product, as I knew I eventually would. And, two, we moved and became frugal. So when it was time to restock my supply of this cleaning product, I just couldn't justify the cost when there were cheaper options available.

For me, and probably for you too, getting used to different products was the hardest initial change to make when it came time for frugal housecleaning. I wanted to be able to use the products that I was familiar with—but, frankly, I'd never paid attention to how much they cost. By cutting out those pricey items, plus a really bad paper-towel habit, and replacing them with either store-brand cleaners or cleaning products I could make at home, I was able to slash my shopping budget and still keep my home tidy and spotless.

Rag Time

During this cleaning metamorphosis, I reached back to my roots and remembered some of the tricks that my Yankee mother had taught me about effective cleaning tools that were essentially free. I remembered how even though we had a sparkling house when I was growing up, my mother didn't use any fancy cleaning tools—not even basic stuff like sponges and mops! No, when my mother needed to clean, her go-to tools were always rags.

My mom favored rags because:

- They were free. These were old T-shirts and towels we otherwise would have thrown out.
- They were reusable. She could just toss them in the washing machine when done with her chores, and then use them again the next time she needed to clean.

- They were recyclable. When the rags became too threadbare to use anymore, my mom would shred the rags and toss them in the compost pile.

Soon after adopting my frugal lifestyle, I adopted my mother's rag-using habit. I started to scour the laundry for T-shirts that were past their prime, or bath towels that had become so worn out that they were too embarrassing to put out when guests visited. Soon enough, I had all the rags a frugal gal could want.

Here's how you can find free rags around your house, too. Each time you do a load of laundry this week, take a really critical look at your husband's undershirts, your kids' old sports T-shirts, and any hand towels or bath towels that are simply beyond their prime. Start putting them aside so that the next time you need to clean something, you can forgo the paper towels and use your free cleaning rags instead.

The key to using rags is making sure that you keep them in a convenient place so using them doesn't become a big hassle. If they aren't in an easy-to-access place, you might fall back on your paper towel habit, which, as you know, costs money.

To decide where to put your rags, consider where you use them most. You might keep a main rag bin in a convenient place with plenty of storage—maybe the garage, mudroom, or basement—with satellite rag stashes in the laundry room, in the kitchen, and under the sink in the master bathroom.

Frugal Cleaners

The cost of cleaning products can add up quickly when you think about what you purchase regularly—window cleaner, bathroom cleaner, floor cleaner, rug cleaners . . . the list goes on and on. To live frugally, I'm sticking with two kinds of cleaners:

the concentrated kind that you can buy in gigantic bottles and add water to and cleaners you make yourself.

CLEANERS YOU CAN MAKE YOURSELF

Some DIY cleaners include:

- Vinegar and baking soda to clear plumbing clogs.
- Baking soda as a scouring powder for the tub.
- Vinegar as an all-purpose cleaner, such as for windows, floors, and appliances. (Note: Do not use vinegar on any kind of stone countertops. It will damage them.)
- Laundry detergent, made with borax, washing soda, and ground soap.

For more on making your own cleaners on a frugal budget, please check out Chapter 8, "Becoming a Do-It-Yourselfer" (page 121).

SEAL OF APPROVAL *MICROFIBER CLOTHS*

While I'm a huge fan of using free cleaning tools, I recently discovered that microfiber cloths are a worthwhile investment for cleaning a frugal home—especially because you can pick up a four-pack of decent-sized cloths (about 12" × 6") at a dollar store for, what else, one dollar.

One of the great things about microfiber cloths is that, like rags, they can be washed and used repeatedly. In addition, they are definitely a multipurpose cleaning tool.

Here are some uses we've discovered for them:

- Clean computer and electronics screens.
- Replace Swiffer-like dusting cloths.

- Wipe down sealed countertop surfaces, such as marble and granite.
- Dust.
- Dry off a dog after a bath.
- Shine and de-fingerprint windows and glass.
- Use in lieu of paper towels.

Here's one way that microfiber cloths beat regular old rags: if you use a mop made for a Swiffer, with push-in holes to grip the cloth, the microfiber cloths stay on easier than T-shirts-as-rags do. The microfiber cloths tend to stay flat on the mop "head" whereas T-shirts-as-rags bunch up as you push them across the floor.

Rags for Good Cause

At some point, you're probably going to find yourself overrun with rags. It is inevitable, especially if you've got kids, who seem to collect T-shirts like rock stars collect groupies. Instead of cluttering up your home with rags you're just never going to use, here's what you can do: donate those would-be rags to an animal rescue organization or shelter. Many of these facilities welcome used (but clean) towels and sheets so they can line cages and pens.

For those who don't already have a plethora of rags like I do, I would recommend picking up a couple of packs of microfiber cloths at the dollar store to get your frugal cleaning started. Given the versatility of microfiber cloths, they've definitely earned my Suddenly Frugal Seal of Approval.

Doing Laundry

When we decided to start living frugally, I made two big changes in how I approached the laundry:

1. I made everyone wear clothing more than once (if possible).
2. I tried to stop relying on the dryer.

These two methods alone are huge energy- and money-savers in the laundry department.

Doing Laundry Less Often

I've changed my approach to frequently washing clothes for two reasons. One, doing fewer and shorter loads of laundry can help cut our energy bills. And, two, our clothes will last longer if they're washed less often. And if they last longer, I can go for extended periods of time when I don't have to spend money on new clothes.

Plus, when you think about it, this notion of wearing clothes more than once makes a lot of sense. Unless you've been rolling in the dirt or have gotten sweaty, there's no reason to automatically throw something in the laundry. Underwear, socks, and sports uniforms? Yeah, they can go right into the hamper at the end of the day. But shirts, sweaters, sweatshirts, pants, and the like? Unless they are noticeably dirty, smelly, or downright gross, fold them back up and put them away in your dresser or closet for another day. Surely you can go a couple of wearings without washing a pair of jeans. Is anyone really going to notice?

If you have kids, you might not be able to have them reuse clothes quite so much. Of course, I can get away with having my whole family follow this rule because my kids are older and aren't outside playing in the dirt, or dropping food on themselves because they're just learning how to use utensils. If you have younger kids, you might not save as many loads of laundry, but it's still a tip worth trying. Every little bit counts.

The idea of rewearing clothes was something my mother tried to drum into me when I was a preteen, and now I'm trying it with my own kids. But guess what I've figured out? You can nag everyone to keep their relatively clean clothes out of the laundry, and then get frustrated when they don't listen to you. Or, when you find something that could easily be worn again, you can just pluck it from the hamper, fold it up with the clean laundry, and put it "away" back in that person's room. No one is the wiser.

Use the Dryer Less Often

If you're trying to be more frugal with your dryer, the most important secret to keep in mind actually has to do with the washing machine: the spin cycle. Clothes dry faster if they're not saturated with water, and the best way to get as much water out of your clothes is to use the spin cycle. Think of it as your laundry centrifuge that spins the water molecules right out of the fabric. (My apologies to Mr. Hamilton, my eleventh grade science teacher, for this oversimplification of how a centrifuge works.) So make sure you're not rushing your clothes into the dryer before the spin cycle is 100 percent completed.

Here are some other ways that you can start to use the dryer less often.

DRY FOR SHORT PERIODS OF TIME ONLY

If you have just washed clothes that you plan on hanging up to dry, try tossing those items in the dryer for, say, ten minutes only. This little bit of time will help to dewrinkle these articles of clothing and get any excess water out of them. I've found that this trick helps make the clothes softer and smoother when I hang them up to dry. Have you ever pulled a wet pair of jeans out of the washing machine and then hung them up to dry? They're kind of crunchy when they do eventually dry, and I gotta tell you, I'm no fan of crunchy jeans. Neither are my kids.

DRY SMALLER LOADS

By pulling clothes out of the dryer one by one, you end up with fewer articles in the dryer overall. And that means that the drying cycle won't have to run as long to get everything dry. Since I draw the line at hanging up underwear and socks, these are usually all that's left in the dryer. Because they're smaller and lighter, socks and underwear usually dry faster without bulky items in the dryer with them. If there are only a few of these lighter items left in the dryer, I'll turn the dryer off completely, and wait until the next load of laundry to turn it back on.

HANG CLOTHES TO DRY OR USE A DRYING RACK

So this last idea isn't dryer dependent, but if you are able to hang your clothes out to dry or can use a drying rack, that is a great option. Personally, I can't line-dry clothes outside because of my pollen allergies. But that doesn't stop me from hanging them on hangers in my laundry room.

If you do like to hang up clothes to dry, here's a tip on the hanger front: when you buy a new article of clothing, ask if you can keep the clear-plastic hanger that the store had used to hang up the item. They'll usually say yes and give you the hanger for free. (Yeah, I love free.)

I've found it's worth it to ask for these hangers because the store ones have ridges on them, which help grip the shirt you hang on it and keep it from falling off. Plus, with the way those hangers are shaped, you can usually avoid those lumps on the shoulders—you know, those telltale signs of something that's been hung on a hanger the wrong way. Also, try to get store pant hangers because those clasps are perfect for hanging up all kinds of bottoms—sweatpants, jeans, and shorts, to name a few.

You may be wondering why I haven't suggested using clothespins. I'm not a huge fan of them, because I've always found that they leave obvious indentations on clothes after drying. Sheets and towels with notches on them are no big deal. But I'd rather avoid clip marks on the bottoms of my shirts, thank you very much.

Cooking Meals

The biggest frugal change we've made with regard to cooking meals is that we're actually making them at home. Before frugality, we'd cook from time to time, but most often we would rely on take-out Chinese or take-in pizza to get the family fed. And as you can imagine, those seemingly inexpensive meals added up over time.

These days, cooking isn't the exception—it's the rule. And when I say "cooking," I don't just mean meals that we heat up for dinner. I'm talking about working hard to make sure that our three squares a day originate at home. This helps us to keep our spending in check, and it's healthier for everyone. Because if meals don't originate at home, they might come from a fast-food restaurant, a vending machine, or a convenience store—locations not exactly known for their nutritional options.

Meal-Planning Prep

One of the ways that we're meeting our cook-at-home goals is through meal planning. Once a week, my husband and I will sit down and brainstorm what we can serve for dinner in the coming days. This brainstorming usually coincides with planning a food-shopping trip, which involves the following:

1. Updating the grocery list. We keep our list stuck on the refrigerator, so that as we run out of grocery items, we can add them right to the list. As we decide on what to eat, we add necessary ingredients to the list.
2. Reading the supermarket circular, which arrives in the mail every Wednesday. We'll go through it and compare it with the grocery list. If certain items we like are on sale—such as last week's drumsticks for $.99 a pound—I plan to stock up and keep anything we won't use this week in my freezer for another dinner down the road.
3. Checking for coupons. I crosscheck coupons not only with my grocery-shopping list but also with what is available on sale at the supermarket that day.
4. Checking the pantry. Of course, it's important to check your pantry, cupboards, freezer, and refrigerator before you head out to the store so you don't buy something you already have. In addition, you can figure out whether, along with the items on your grocery list and what's on sale at the supermarket, your pantry will provide all the ingredients you need for the coming week's meals.

Keep in mind that our prepping for grocery shopping also includes making sure that we've got enough "supplies" on hand for breakfasts every morning—including my beloved coffee, which I'm brewing at home each morning now. Plus, we need to be sure we have food for the lunches our girls take to school or camp every day.

Meal Planning in Action

When it comes time to do the meal planning, we try to keep things simple. We'll just jot down a list of things we could have for dinner. We don't assign meals to certain nights, unless we know that we're going to have a particularly busy afternoon with kids' sports and other commitments. In our prefrugal life, these were the nights when we would just call the local pizza joint, and call it dinner. But with our planning these days, I just make sure that I've got everything I need to simplify eating dinner at home on busy nights.

For example, recently we had a jam-packed afternoon that would leave us only about an hour between getting home from school and work and our having to be back out the door again for some other commitment. At 7:00 that morning, while the kids were eating breakfast, I was prepping chicken drumsticks for the Crock-Pot so that they could cook all day and be ready for dinner.

On another day when I knew our evening would be busy, because my daughter had a softball game at 6:00 that night, I marinated chicken breasts in the morning and let them sit all day. When the workday was over, I threw the breasts on the grill and then, while they cooked, I cut up some fruit and vegetables, put them in reusable containers, and stashed them in a cooler. When the chicken was done, I put them in sandwich buns, wrapped them in aluminum foil and tossed them in the cooler, too. Finally, I filled our refillable water bottles with H20, and we were out the door and on our way to the field—with dinner in tow—in no time flat. That's how you have to think about your schedule ahead of time in order to avoid expensive takeout meals.

Here's another meal-planning trick we use besides the planning ahead based on what our calendar looks like: I always try to cook extra food with leftovers in mind. This helps in two ways.

1. It gives me a night when I don't have to start from scratch with dinner. For example, that night when I grilled chicken to eat at the softball field, I made more than we needed and served the leftovers cold over a bed of lettuce the next night.
2. If we have a night when we know we'll be arriving home late from sports or other commitments, we can easily reheat a meal. This has helped cut down on the temptation of stopping on the way home for McFood.

There are two additional reasons that meal planning will improve your quality of life, even though you're trying to live frugally.

The first reason is this: it will reduce your weeknight stress or the feared five o'clock "what are we having for dinner" question that often hangs over us. You know those nights—you're exhausted from the day, everyone is hungry, and you just don't know what to serve for dinner so you order in. Nope, not going to do that anymore. You will feel freer and less stressed knowing exactly which meals are coming down the pike, or at least which meals you have the supplies on hand to make.

The second reason is that with meal planning, you will be setting the stage so that your family will be able to sit down together each night to enjoy dinner. I don't have to rattle off any statistics about how eating meals with parents helps kids or how eating together can keep a marriage strong. I'm pretty sure you can figure that out for yourself once you start reaping the benefits of meal planning and family meals eaten together. I mean, who knew that in trying to save your family money and do some meal planning that you could improve your relationships as well? That's so cool.

Managing the Takeout Temptation

Just because we try to be frugal when it comes to eating, we don't "deny" ourselves takeout foods. We instead make takeout-like meals at home.

For example, one day last summer, our refrigerator was overflowing with vegetables—green peppers, onions, and broccoli. I could almost taste all of those delicious vegetables simmering on top of a freshly made pizza, but I sure as heck didn't want to spend $20 or more for a couple of veggie-topped pies from the pizzeria. I did end up stopping at the local pizza joint but not to order those pies—no, I didn't give in to temptation. Instead, I picked up two lumps of pizza dough ($6) so that with sauce I had in the pantry and mozzarella cheese I had in the refrigerator—and the aforementioned veggies, of course—we could make DIY pizzas at home.

Eventually I'll learn how to make pizza dough that's as delicious as the pizza guy's dough so I can save the $6. But until then, I'm okay with this little splurge because we still get to eat our pizza and save $14 on a meal.

Stocking Up When There's a Sale

Buying items only when they're on sale and when you have a coupon, too, is a quick win in the frugal department. Case in point: Recently I stocked up on crescent rolls. We are always using crescent rolls in one way or another at dinner. I use them for a makeshift version of *pain au chocolat* (just sprinkle chocolate chips and a little bit of sugar inside the crescent-roll dough, roll up, and bake normally) for a quick homemade dessert. I also use crescent rolls as the base for my "breakfast pizza," which we actually serve at dinner (the crescent rolls are the crust, over which I pour beaten eggs with milk, and then sprinkle bacon pieces and shredded cheese on top. Then into the oven it goes). Or there are some nights when we'd just like to have dinner rolls with our meal.

Printing Out Coupons

You probably already know that you should be scouring your Sunday newspaper for coupons. But did you know that you can also find coupons online for offline shopping? At first I thought the supermarket wouldn't accept coupons that I'd printed at home, because of fraud. But the coupons you can get from websites these days come with bar codes that scan just like the coupons you find in the newspaper. Recently, I downloaded and printed a $2-off coupon from Coupons.com (*www.coupons.com*) for a Del Monte whole pineapple. Luckily, those pineapples were on sale at my supermarket that week for $2.49, meaning I was able to secure a fresh whole pineapple for only forty-nine cents. Besides Coupons.com, here are two other coupons sites worth visiting for printable coupons: Coupon Winner (*www.couponwinner.com*) and Coupon Mom (*www.couponmom.com*).

Anyway, one week my grocery store had both the Pillsbury version of crescent rolls on sale along with the store-brand version, but I had a coupon for the Pillsbury brand, which made this sale too good to resist. With my doubled coupon and some quick math in the refrigerator aisle, I figured out that while the store-brand version, on sale, was $1.50 per package, with my coupon and the sale price combined, the Pillsbury version was $1.43 per package. I'm sure you can guess which brand I purchased.

And I did what I always do when I find a great deal on something that I regularly use—I stocked up. I had four coupons I could use to save on eight packages of crescent rolls, and that's exactly what I did.

I also stock up when there are sales on staples such as pasta (a buck a box or less) or sandwich bread. Whenever my grocery store runs its ten loaves for $10 deal, I'll usually take those ten loaves and pop nine of them in the freezer for sandwich making in the near future. I'll keep one loaf out for that week's sandwiches.

These super deals are cyclical. Though it's difficult to figure out exactly when they come around, they always do. So try to stock up when the price is right. Your supplies will probably hold up until those super deals appear again.

Chest Freezers = Cha-Ching?

My grandparents, who lived in rural Maine, always had their chest freezer fully stocked. This was in addition to their pantry and regular refrigerator and freezer. Having this backup cold storage was a must for them, since they lived miles from the nearest grocery store, and my grandfather hunted and needed a place to store his meat. But even if you live around the corner from the supermarket and get your meat in the butcher department, you may find a chest freezer to be a worthwhile investment.

Costing between $200 and $700, chest freezers allow you to stock up on produce, meats, bread, and more when they're on sale. You can even freeze milk for up to three months—good to know if your kids drink a lot and you find milk at a can't-beat-it price. Chest freezers range in size from five cubic feet to eighteen cubic feet (that's the interior space), and, according to the Energy Star website, chest freezers are the most energy-efficient freezer you can buy. *Consumer Reports* says that chest freezers are also a good idea if you live somewhere that's prone to power outages, because they can keep what's inside colder longer than upright refrigerator/freezer combinations.

A chest freezer would make sense if your regular refrigerator and freezer simply can't hold everything you need to store cold. When my supermarket has bread on sale for $1 a loaf, I'm usually limited to buying only the number of loaves I can fit into my top freezer. As I mentioned above, I'm lucky enough to be able to fit the ten that are on sale in the $10 for ten loaves deal. If I had a chest freezer, I could probably buy many more loaves at once. As long as the bread was still very fresh when I bought it and put it in the freezer, I could feel confident that it would be good enough to eat when I thawed it up to six months down the road. So if you're looking for a way to store large quantities of food purchased at a discount, a chest freezer might make sense for you.

Drinks on the House

You may not even realize how much your family spends on drinks—juice, soda, and so on. While you clearly want to maintain a healthy, balanced diet, your family can probably make some sacrifices for the sake of frugality. Here are two ideas.

DRINK FREE WATER!

Probably the easiest change you can make with regard to eating and frugality is to cut back on buying nonessential drinks and start drinking more water. And that would be the stuff that you can get for free out of your faucet. We've gotten so used to drinking bottled water in this country, because we've been led to believe that it tastes better and is better for us. I think that's just money down the drain.

If you really don't like the way the water that comes out of your tap tastes, invest in a sink-mounted water filter, or get a water filtration system in your refrigerator—assuming your fridge is equipped for one. We have a faucet-mount Brita filter that gives us delicious water (*www.brita.com*). Because the water coming out of the faucet isn't always as cold as we'd like, we also keep a pitcher of filtered water in the refrigerator. (You can also get Brita-filtered pitchers for water.) This saves us money on our water bill, because we no longer have to leave the water running in the sink until it's cold enough for a glass. Want some flavor to your tap water? Add a splash of juice and save yourself the money on flavored waters.

Also, get yourself out of the habit of buying bottles of water when you're out and about and you find yourself thirsty. Instead, plan ahead and bring along a bottle of water in a reusable container. It's rare that you'll find me out running errands or attending a meeting without my trusted Nalgene refillable bottle with me. This way, if I do find myself parched, I don't spend money on water I could get for free at home, I'm not creating waste with a disposable bottle, and I drink my daily dose of water to stay hydrated.

SEAL OF APPROVAL *MAKE YOUR OWN CARBONATED DRINKS WITH A SODASTREAM*

Here's another cost savings I've discovered: making my own seltzer as opposed to buying it in bottles or cans at the supermarket. Originally, I was taken with this idea of DIY seltzer for more green (to avoid using all those bottles and cans) than frugal reasons. But eventually frugal won out.

Because I love drinking seltzer—it gives me the fizz I crave from soda without the bone-damaging effects some research says colas cause—I was going through two to four one-liter bottles of seltzer a week. At fifty cents a pop from the supermarket, this wasn't too expensive an indulgence, but it did add up. Two bucks a week times fifty-two weeks, and you're looking at a $100-a-year habit.

Packing Frugal Lunches

If you want to be truly frugal, you need to start packing lunch every day—whether for you to bring to work or for your kids to bring to school. Invest in reusable containers that you can keep in daily rotation for lunches. My family uses these kinds of containers to hold chips, crackers, and cut-up fruit. In addition, another reusable container that is well worth the investment is a sandwich holder (dishwasher-safe plastic boxes perfectly sized for sandwiches). Check out products such as the Sandwich Keeper from Tupperware (*www.tupperware.com*) or square TakeAlongs containers from Rubbermaid (*www.rubbermaid.com*). And then don't forget about reusable water bottles for drinks. You can also find inexpensive stainless steel bottles at most stores; recently we picked up a bunch for under $5 each at Old Navy (*www.oldnavy.com*).

Then there was the issue of all the waste: I was tossing four plastic bottles a week into my recycling bin. And if you know anything about the abysmal recycling record for plastic bottles, then you know that those bottles likely ended up in landfills rather than recycled. It's just the way it is. So I decided that I needed to figure out a way that I could still enjoy my seltzer without spending too much or sending too many plastic bottles to landfill purgatory. That's why for a one-time fee of $100, I got a SodaStream soda maker machine.

This countertop machine (about the height of a medium-sized fire extinguisher) comes with reusable, one-liter bottles that you fill with tap water (filtered, if you'd like) and then attach to the Sodastream machine. With the push of a button, the machine adds carbon dioxide (read: bubbles, carbonation, fizzies) to your water, and now you've got seltzer. You can pay extra to get syrups to make sodas with the machine, too, but I'll usually drink the seltzer straight with a slice of lemon or lime in it, or I'll add a dash of my kids' cranberry-grape juice for some flavor.

If you're interested in making your own seltzer, visit the SodaStream website: *www.sodaclubusa.com.*

Make It Good to the Last Drop

A truly frugal person tries not to let anything go to waste. That means that when you think your supplies of a certain item are almost done, you need to do whatever you can to stretch that item's usefulness for a little longer to save money.

Here's how to put this idea to work: when your hair conditioner or shampoo is running low in the shower, fill the bottle one-quarter of the way with water, put the top back on, and give it a good shake. I'll bet you'll have at least a week's worth of conditioner left, thanks to that added water. Do the same with liquid hand soap, dishwashing liquid, and even the extra bit of tomato sauce left in the jar. (Some of my friends add a little wine to the water to swish around in a tomato sauce jar to add a bit of flavor without watering down the sauce too much.)

With other kinds of food, get out your rubber spatula. I use mine to swipe the last few tablespoons of peanut butter from the jar, or for getting the rest of the batter in a bowl when I'm making a cake, waffles, or pancakes. In fact, recently when making pancakes, you would have thought that I didn't have enough batter left in the bowl for any more breakfast. But one revolution around the mixing bowl with my rubber spatula turned up enough batter for an additional pancake, which I promptly cooked. And to think that without my rubber spatula, I'd have thrown away a perfectly good pancake.

If you have a tube of something that's running low—and you just can't get another drop out of it—try this: get out a pair of scissors and snip off the flat end of the tube. I know plenty of frugalistas who can squeeze out a few more days' worth of eye cream, lip gloss, or toothpaste from a seemingly empty tube, just by cutting off the end. If you can't cut off an end, try dipping a Q-Tip into the tube—assuming the mouth is wide enough—to scrape the bottom of the barrel, so to speak.

Finally, when it doubt, turn a bottle upside down and let it sit overnight. Whether it's ketchup, concealer, or creamy dressing, gravity will help you shake down a bottle so you can get a few more uses before you have to spend money to buy new.

Everyday Expenses

I'd mentioned how I always make sure to have coffee supplies on hand, now that I'm brewing my coffee at home. This has been a tremendous help for our family to live more frugally. I figured out that I'm saving about $1,000 a year in coffee spending.

In fact, I recently read a survey that says the average American drinks 1,132 cups of coffee each year, and that the average price of a cup of coffee is $1.38. Now, I don't know about you, but unless you're buying the smallest size coffee possible and going to a bargain-basement coffeehouse, you're going to spend way more than $1.38 for a cup of coffee.

Here's another way that we've cut down on our everyday expenses: every six months or so, we'll sit down and review our bills and credit card charges. During this review we look for costs we can take a scalpel to so we can save money in the long run.

Last year we figured out that we were spending about $65 a month (or about $750 a year) on a second landline in the house. I used that landline as my dedicated phone number for my writing business, but over the years I'd been using that phone line less in favor of my cell phone. I realized that if I cut my landline, we'd save some serious dough. So we made that cut.

Recently, we sat down again to review our bills, and this time we took aim at the single remaining landline in our home. Again, it cost about $750 a year to keep. While we weren't interested in getting rid of that line altogether, we were curious to know how switching phone providers might save us money. We looked into different phone companies as well as our cable provider to see which one made the most sense financially. And in the end we decided to take advantage of our cable company's "triple play" program, which puts your cable TV, Internet, and phone service all on the same bill.

That switch was seamless as far as the phone service goes, but here's where the benefits have kicked in. We're saving $50 a month on phone service, which adds up to $600 a year. And because of a special the cable company was running—a permanent special, not just something that lasts three months only—we were able to get back some premium cable channels, which we'd cut out on the road to frugality. This time around we wouldn't have to pay anything extra for these channels. I know that having these premium channels back will help us save money on our movie fixes, a topic I discuss in Chapter 5, "Mixing Media with Frugality."

Total Savings in This Chapter

We covered a lot of ground in this chapter about how you can change your daily habits and routines when you embrace frugality. And I hope you've come to see that you really don't have to make huge sacrifices in order to save money. Instead, think of them as smart decisions that will benefit your bottom line.

Possible savings in Chapter 1: $2,400

chapter two

SHIFTING HOW YOU SHOP

When looking at life through a frugal lens, you realize that shopping for clothing, groceries, and supplies has to take on a whole new meaning. You still need to get what your family needs to survive, but you have to change how you get those things, how frequently you buy them, and how much you spend on them.

That's why this chapter uncovers deals to be had online, making the most of back-to-school shopping, the benefits of hand-me-downs, and looking for locally grown produce—even if it's "locally grown" in your own backyard! This chapter will also show you how you can reuse certain objects in new ways so you'll save money in the long run.

Clothing

These days, it takes a lot for me to justify buying new clothes. I've never been much of a fashion follower but that doesn't mean that I don't like to have nice things from time to time. However, when you're living frugally, you can't just go out and buy the latest (fill in the blank) because that's what everyone is wearing. But it doesn't mean you have to look sloppy or unfashionable either. My trick to feeling current is buying high-quality classics, and treating my clothes well so that they last a long time. Then I can simply update my wardrobe a few pieces at a time when I come across a great deal.

Be Patient

For example, after watching episode after episode of *What Not to Wear,* I realized that I really needed a casual blazer or short jacket that I could use to dress up an everyday outfit. So I became laser-focused on finding an affordable blazer that was well-made and looked great on me—and, of course, didn't cost too much. I started scouring the sale racks at every store I visited, and eventually, months after my quest began, I hit design pay dirt.

At a Goodwill location in New England (*www.goodwillnne.org*), of all places, I found a fitted blue corduroy blazer from American Eagle. Sure, it was gently used and needed a good ironing, but it fit me perfectly and cost only $6.99. Be still my frugal heart. I know this casual blazer will become a staple in my wardrobe, and that it's going to last me a long time because it is a classic from a reputable company known for its well-made clothes.

It wasn't easy waiting so long to find this piece of clothing, but curing myself of impulse shopping wasn't easy either. However, I knew that in order to cut down on my spending, I had to cut down on shopping on the fly. One of the ways I was able to overcome the impulse to spend was to stay out of the stores altogether where I would likely overspend. The other was to recognize and remember my feelings of buyer's remorse. That's the nagging in the pit of your stomach when you've purchased something that you know you shouldn't have. Once I could recall how rotten that all felt, I didn't want to feel that way again, and I no longer felt the overwhelming need to shop, shop, shop.

Stock Up During Sales

Besides finding that one piece you've been searching for, consider stocking up on clothing basics when you find them on sale—the same way you would with your groceries. Soup's on sale for pennies apiece? I'm taking as many cans as I can carry. Underwear is on clearance? I'm all over that! New undies for everyone! The key is to stick to basic items you know you'll like and wear for a long time.

For example, my most consistent clothing stockup occurs around two items from Gap *(www.gap.com)*. I'm a huge fan of Gap's Favorite long-sleeved shirts, which are a staple of my winter wardrobe, as are Gap's ribbed undershirts. So if I happen to see them on sale in a store or via Gap.com, I'll re-up my supplies—even if it's the middle of summer. I find that doing this every two years gives me enough shirts on hand that I can wear on a daily basis without spending too much money overall.

Shop at Outlets

Another way you can score great clothing deals is to shop at outlets. Granted, outlet shopping is nothing like what it was even a few years ago. Then, stores sent their overstocks to the outlets, where they would mark them down like crazy just to move the inventory. These days many stores produce clothing lines exclusively for outlet stores, and they don't always discount these prices.

Nonetheless, you can still find bargains at the outlets if you know what to look for and how to shop. Here are four tips for not going off your budget when shopping for clothes at the outlets.

1. Shop in tax-free states. Okay, so this advice applies to regular clothing shopping, too. But it will be like getting a double discount if you can get a great deal on clothing at an outlet and you happen to be shopping in a state that doesn't tax clothing purchases—states such as New Hampshire, New Jersey, and Pennsylvania. Also, keep in mind that Alaska, Delaware, Montana, and Oregon do not charge sales tax of any kind. If you live in a state that normally taxes clothing purchases, check out this website that lists tax-free shopping holidays: *www.taxadmin.org/fta/rate/sales_holiday.html.*
2. Buy when you find a bargain on something you need, not just because you found it at an outlet store. I think that too often you can fall into thinking that just because you're shopping at an outlet, you are automatically getting a great bargain. This is not always true. As I mentioned above, lots of times the clothes at outlets are made just for the outlets. They're not the super-secret clearance items from the main stores. So this means that when you find yourself shopping at an outlet store, make sure you're making a purchase based on an item you like, believe would add value to your wardrobe (or home, depending on what you're considering purchasing), and is truly a good deal.
3. Shop with a plan in mind. Just as a smart shopper goes to the grocery store with a list in hand, you should approach an outlet-shopping trip with a purpose in mind. The best way to keep your spending within limits is to shop off of your list and not to make any last-minute, impulse purchases that you

didn't budget for. So even though you might feel silly making a shopping list for clothing, go ahead and do it. I'll bet it will help you keep your spending on track, even if it means you leave the outlets having bought nothing at all. That's a good thing, too! It means you didn't just mindlessly shop, or engage in shopper-tainment. And you most certainly won't walk away feeling that awful buyer's remorse.

4. Know your return options before buying anything. In most retail situations, as long as you have a receipt to prove that you bought something at a store, you can return that item for a refund or exchange. While many stores have time limits for returns, basically as long as you have a receipt and the tags on your clothing, you shouldn't have too much trouble taking something back. Well, things aren't that easy when you shop at an outlet. Sometimes clothing purchased at an outlet is "final sale," and sometimes it must be returned to the outlet—not the name-brand store somewhere else. I learned this lesson the hard way once when I bought something at the Gap outlet, and then tried to return it at the Gap store in the mall. Nope, I had to go back to an outlet to make my return. So buyer (and returner) beware.

Take Advantage of Deals at Thrift and Consignment Shops

While we've done back-to-school shopping at the outlets in the past, the truth is we try to pick up new clothing all summer long, when we have coupons or stores are having sales. And we like to round out any necessary clothing purchases by shopping at thrift and consignment stores whenever possible.

Also, because we make our daughters spend their own money on what we deem "frivolous" clothing purchases, they have learned that they can really stretch their bucks when they buy used clothing at stores such as teen-oriented resale franchise Plato's Closet (*www.platoscloset.com*). This is where my fashion-conscious tween was able to pick up the Abercrombie, American Eagle, and Hollister labels she covets without paying full price. And my graphic-tee-loving teen was able to find vintage-looking T-shirts for just a few dollars each.

If you're interested in adding thrift or consignment shopping to your frugal ways of shopping for clothing, consider these eight tips.

1. Look for recognizable brands. Buying brand-name items in a thrift store can be beneficial in two ways. One, if you've worn this brand before, you know how it fits. And two, if you're familiar with the brand and know that it's well made, you know that you're likely to get more wear out of this item than a cheaper version over the long run.
2. Understand that shopping thrift doesn't always mean used clothing. Last summer my daughter found a brand new Aeropostale skort on sale for $5 at Goodwill. The skort still had the tags on it. The summer before that, I picked up a Gap sherbet-green wool, fully lined pea coat at a church thrift store. It, too, still had the tags on it. Instead of spending $50, which is what the tags had told me it had retailed for at the Gap, I got it for $.50 (I'm not kidding).
3. Even thrift stores have sales. Each day of the week, Goodwill puts certain items on sale. You'll know what those items are based on the color of the plastic tag on the garment. So one day everything with an orange plastic tag could be 20 percent off whereas the next day items with a blue plastic tag will be 20 percent off. Saving extra money on already affordable items is a definite win in my book.

4. Some thrift stores have outlet locations. Did you know that the Goodwills of the world have thrift store outlets? These are the kinds of places where the merchandise that these stores really can't sell goes to die—or gets sold at heavily discounted prices. Some of these outlets sell clothes by the pound, which may not make a lot of sense for your everyday shopping. However, if you're a seamstress or knitter—or your teen is a would-be *Project Runway* contestant, always on the lookout for supplies to make new outfits with—then getting clothing by the pound like this would seem to be the best deal out there! Just do a Google search for "Goodwill outlet" to see if there is one located near you. As of this writing there are about twenty-five outlet locations nationwide, including stores in the Seattle area, Indianapolis, Portland (Oregon), Nashville, and the San Francisco area.
5. Haggle to your heart's content. If I'm shopping in a regular store and I find something wrong with a garment—and there aren't any other garments like it left to choose—I have no problem bringing that garment to the register, pointing out the damage, and then asking "So what can you do for me?" Usually, I can get 10 percent or 20 percent knocked off the price of an item. Turns out that you can use the same haggling techniques at thrift stores, too. True, you're probably already getting something for a good price. But it doesn't hurt to point out if a button is missing or there's lipstick on a shirt—if you know that you can replace the button or clean off the lipstick when you get home. Why not see if you can get a little more money off of your purchase?
6. Dress the part for trying on clothes while thrift shopping. The one downside of thrift stores is that they don't always have generous dressing rooms—if any dressing rooms at all. That's why whenever I decide to go shopping for clothes at a

thrift store, I make sure I wear fitted clothing that will allow me to try other things on over it. (I learned this trick from shopping at New York City sample sales.)

7. Know the real price of things before buying. Just as you can get tricked into thinking that anything that's on sale at an outlet is a good deal, you can easily fall into the same trap at a thrift store. So be prepared to shop around a bit if you're looking for something specific, like that blazer I wanted. When I found that perfect American Eagle blazer for $6.99, I knew it was a good deal and had no qualms buying it.
8. Don't expect great return policies at thrift stores. One of the ways that thrift stores keep prices low and make money for the good causes they support is keeping their overhead low. And they do that by not having elaborate return policies. Most sales are final sales, which means you really need to think hard about buying something if you know you can't return it. It's kind of like going to a garage sale. You have to ask yourself, *Will I have buyer's remorse the minute I get in the car?* And if you can't return the item, is it worth buying in the first place? If you have any doubts at all, put the item back.

Sell Clothes to Make Money

Perhaps you've noticed new thrift and consignment stores opening up for business in your town. We have three such shops where I live, and all seem to be thriving. According to the National Association of Resale and Thrift Shops (*www.narts.org*), 83 percent of these kinds of stores have seen an increase in new customers coming in to shop in 2009 versus 2008. With more customers through the door, these stores need inventory to sell. So now more than ever, it's a great time to make some extra money by selling your used clothing at a thrift or consignment shop.

One of the benefits of my daughters buying used clothes from a store like Plato's Closet is that they know where to go to sell their used clothing in the future. And given that they're always looking for ways to earn extra money, this newly discovered option works out very well for them. Recently, we cleaned out their closets and uncovered a number of T-shirts and jeans that we brought to Plato's Closet to sell. First, we checked them for stains, holes, and anything beyond normal wear and tear. Next, we made sure that the clothes were clean and fresh-smelling. Finally, we double-checked that the garments didn't look too old or out of date. If there's one thing we've learned about selling clothing to a hip store like Plato's Closet, it's this: low-rise anything goes fast. (Mom jeans? They're not interested.) Once we'd determined that these clothes were resale-worthy, they brought them in, and walked out later with a few extra bucks in their pockets.

Previously, I'd tried to make money by selling clothes on eBay. Maybe you did, too. And while I was usually successful in getting someone to bid on the clothing I was auctioning, I always dreaded shipping the items and dealing with the costs associated with that—even if the auction price covered it. Now I'm relieved to have thrift stores near me where I can drop off clothes for resale—and hopefully make a little extra money—and not have to worry about the whole shipping mess.

Groceries

One of the best ways I've found to remain frugal in how I shop for groceries is to set a routine and stick to it. It's the same with exercise. I know that every morning when I get up, I get dressed right into my workout gear. That way when the kids leave for school (or camp, depending on the time of year), I can head right out the door for my morning exercise. These days, my husband and I go food shopping together one night a week, and it's become part of our regular routine, too.

Since we both work during the day, the only fair thing seemed to be that we would both go grocery shopping at night. Besides, with two of us in the supermarket, we get through the shopping list, the checkout counter, and putting the groceries away back at home twice as fast.

Plan Before You Shop

Before we head out the door, we do some planning. We talked about this briefly in Chapter 1, but let's get more specific now. We know how important this is because doing food shopping on the fly often leads to overspending. So what do we do as part of our planning?

- Inventory our current supplies in the pantry, refrigerator, and freezer.
- Check our calendar and plan meals according to what we have going on during the evening in the coming week.
- Scan our recipes and cross-check them against our meal plan and our current supplies.
- Review the supermarket circular and tweak meal plans as necessary to match them with items that might be on sale.
- Finalize our shopping list.
- Pull out and organize coupons based on what we've got on our list.

One of the ways that we keep our shopping list organized is by not waiting until the last minute to write it. I have a notepad with a magnetic back that I've stuck to the refrigerator door.

Whenever we run low or out of something in the kitchen, everyone in the family knows to write that item down on the list. On shopping night, I tear off that week's list and use it when we go to the store.

Set Spending Goals

For a long time I've tried to stick to $150 a week for groceries. In reality that number has crept up to $180—perhaps because of some laziness on my part or maybe because, in reality, things simply cost more this year than last.

When you decide as a family how much money to spend each week or month for necessities, you tend to be more diligent in how you spend that money. That's how we came up with the $150 benchmark. Revisit these goals quarterly to see what is working and what is not. It was during one of these revisits that we realized our benchmark had crept up to $180.

Handheld Scanners

Some supermarkets now offer handheld scanners to their shoppers. This device lets shoppers scan the items in their cart before getting to the checkout counter, so they save time and know up-front how much they will likely spend on their grocery shopping. I wish my grocery store was this up on technology, because I would love to be able to use this tool to keep my spending in check long before the cashier tells me the total amount that I owe. If you happen to grocery shop at a supermarket that offers handheld scanners to its customers, try one the next time you're in the store and have a few minutes to figure it out. I'll bet it will be an additional way to rein in your spending and keep your food purchases on budget.

Buy Grocery Store Gift Cards

Even with goals, it's never too late to try a new approach to a common chore like food shopping in order to save money. That's why recently my husband and I tried to limit our grocery spending to $600 for the month. And here's how we did that: On the first of the month, we purchased six $100 gift cards to the grocery store. Then on that and subsequent trips to the store, we used only the gift cards to cover our purchases. When the money ran out, we were done shopping for the month, and we had to make do with "clean out the cupboard" kinds of meals. You would be surprised at how much food you actually have in the house, even when you think there's nothing to eat.

Have Store Smarts

We've already established that having a game plan in place, such as meals and a shopping list, can help keep your spending on track at the supermarket. Here are two things I want you to *avoid* or else you might end up spending more than planned.

1. Remember what your mom always told you, and don't go food shopping when you're hungry. That really is a recipe for overspending. When your tummy is growling, the bakery department will seem irresistible, those samples they're giving out (with a coupon!) will become must-buys for you, and anything you're craving on your empty stomach will suddenly end up in your shopping cart.
2. If at all possible, leave the kids at home. I try to avoid taking my I-want-it-now kids with me when I go food shopping, because they always seem to convince me to buy items I don't have on my list. Plus, I'm less likely to focus on cost comparisons and label reading if I'm trying to rush through

the store with kids in tow. Kids plus mom at the supermarket? Nobody wins.

Use Your Kitchen Tools to Save Money on Groceries

If there's one thing that food manufacturers know, it's this: if they can make a product convenient for us, we're probably going to buy it. Never mind that convenience comes at a price—literally. Many of today's time-starved families are willing to pay more to get dinner on the table faster. But when you're trying to live more frugally, something has got to give. In my mind, the easiest thing to go are those prepackaged foods that scream convenience. That's why I believe in using your kitchen tools to make your grocery shopping more budget-friendly. Yes, it may take you a little longer to prepare some ingredients, but you can use the time to catch up with your family or watch the news.

CHEESE SHREDDER

How often do you buy shredded cheese to use in tacos, sprinkle on lasagna, or melt in a tortilla? Did you ever stop to think about how much more you're paying for a package of shredded cheese? I'll bet you have a cheese shredder in your kitchen. Why aren't you using it?

While cheese itself isn't cheap, until you've compared the per-pound price of cheese in its various forms, you probably have no idea how different the prices can be based on what form the cheese is in. Recently at the store, the unit price of an eight-ounce bag of finely shredded mozzarella cheese was $7. (The unit was price per pound.) The unit price for a sixteen-ounce block of mozzarella cheese was $4. When you do the math, the results are significant. Sixteen ounces of the already shredded mozzarella cheese cost $7. But if I took home sixteen ounces of cheese and shredded it myself, it cost only $4. Right there I saved $3 on my grocery bill.

SEAL OF APPROVAL *KITCHEN SHEARS*

It didn't dawn on me how kitchen shears, those spring-loaded scissors made for cutting meat, could help save me money until one day when I was in the butcher department at the supermarket. I noticed that chicken tenderloins were on "sale." I put that in quotes because the sale price wasn't very cheap at all—they were about $3.99 a pound. When regular chicken breasts are on sale, I can get them for as cheap as $1.19 a pound.

Though the tenderloins would be awfully convenient for making fajitas or another dish where I need strips of chicken, here's what I figured out: as long as I have kitchen shears, I never have to buy anything but the cheapest chicken breasts. That's because these kitchen shears allow me to trim chicken breasts into whatever shape, size, or thickness I please.

One night I might trim off a little fat and toss them on the grill. Another night, if we're having fajitas, I'll use the shears to cut the chicken breast into strips. On a night when we're having stir-fry, I'll get out the shears again and cut the chicken breast into chunks. Then, when I'm done with the shears, which are stainless steel and from Pampered Chef (*www.pamperedchef.com*), they can go right into the dishwasher. That makes cleanup a snap.

These shears (which cost me $15 initially) have more than made back their initial investment. They have allowed me flexibility in my kitchen and the ability to keep my spending on meat as low as possible. That's why I'm giving a Suddenly Frugal Seal of Approval to kitchen shears.

SLOW COOKER

One final tool that I think every kitchen should have: a Crock-Pot or slow cooker. In Chapter 3 ("Using Appliances That Don't Suck . . ."), I'll explain how this countertop appliance can help you cook dinner without running up your energy bill. But right now I want to help you understand why a Crock-Pot (*www.crock-pot.com*) can help you maintain a frugal grocery budget and save time, too.

Let's start with the notion of saving time. The beauty of a slow cooker is that you can just toss all of the ingredients—even frozen meat—into the pot, turn it on for six or eight hours, and by the end of the day, you've got a fully cooked meal. You don't have to hassle with defrosting this or thawing that when trying to get dinner on the table. Everything can go into the slow cooker in the morning, and by the time you get home from work, your meal is done.

Now as far as the cost savings go: having a slow cooker on hand ensures that you can use the chicken in your freezer that you stocked up on when it was on sale or the frozen vegetables you snapped up when they were super cheap. Remember: with a slow cooker you can begin cooking the meal while food is still frozen. So you can take your inexpensive ingredients out of the freezer in the morning, put them in the slow cooker, and, as I mentioned before, by the time dinnertime rolls around, you'll have a freshly cooked meal that didn't bust your budget.

Why is this a cost savings over just cooking defrosted food for dinner? Simple: there have been a number of times, in the days before frugality, where I would take something out in the morning to defrost, only to discover at dinnertime that the item was still frozen. Stuck between a rock-solid hunk of frozen meat and a hard place and wondering what to cook for dinner, I usually ended up ordering in, just to get something on the table.

These days, with my trusty slow cooker, I never have to turn to takeout as my fallback plan.

Eat Locally to Eat Frugally

I was always under the impression that fruits and vegetables that you bought at local farms were somehow more expensive than the produce you could get at the supermarket. It wasn't until I crunched some numbers that I realized this: when fruits and vegetables are in season, it's actually cheaper *not* to buy them at the grocery store.

Take apples as an example. A delicious variety here in Pennsylvania is called honey crisp. I can get these apples for less than $1 a pound at my local orchard when they're in season. At my supermarket? They're at least $1.59 a pound when in season and as much as $2.99 when they're out of season. (The apples get shipped in from somewhere else.) Visit *www.localharvest.org* to find farm stands and markets near you for the freshest, most local produce possible.

COMMUNITY SUPPORTED AGRICULTURE (CSA)

Another way of buying locally and saving money is joining a CSA—community supported agriculture farm. (Again, visit the website *www.localharvest.org* to find out about CSA farm options near you.)

At first glance, joining a CSA farm may not seem like such a savings, because, truthfully, they're not cheap. Last year I paid $800 for a full share in my local CSA farm. But get this: that $800 gave me about thirty pounds of fresh fruits and vegetables per week for the six months that the CSA season runs.

When I looked back at my grocery bills when deciding whether or not it was worth it to join the CSA farm, here's what I found: I was spending at least $40 a week on produce at the grocery store. Multiply $40 a week by the twenty-four weeks of a CSA season and you get $960. So right there the CSA membership gave me more value for the money.

Here's another reason a CSA farm is worth the up-front bucks: I'm getting organically grown fruits and vegetables whereas at the supermarket I was just buying "regular" produce. I might spring for organic lettuce or tomatoes every once in a while, but even without spending more for organics, I was spending more overall before joining the CSA farm.

So what's the big deal about the organics? Well, not only are they better for you, but because the produce from a CSA farm is freshly picked, it can last longer than the stuff you would pick up in the supermarket. Whereas regular lettuce from the grocery store would be mush in a week's time, a head of organically grown lettuce from my CSA farm was crisp for at least two weeks. And this was without storage in the crisper or any other special care.

How's this as food for thought—literally? Garlic that was part of the harvest during the last week of the CSA season in November was still fresh and usable for dinners I was cooking in late March. I doubt that a head of garlic grown somewhere clear across the country, and shipped to my grocery store where it would sit for who knows how long, would have held up as long as my locally grown, organic garlic from the CSA farm.

HOW CSA FARMS WORKS

A CSA farm is community supported because people like myself buy a "subscription" to, or shares in, an actual farm. Our annual fees help support the farmers who grow the produce we get to pick up weekly and help ensure that they make a decent living wage.

According to Local Harvest, a website devoted to connecting people with organic and locally grown food, CSA farms are becoming increasingly available and popular to people who want to know where their food is being grown. Fifteen years ago or so, there were only about fifty such farms in the United States. Today, there are more than 1,000.

If you're unfamiliar with how a CSA farm works, here's a brief primer.

For starters, though the growing season begins in the spring, many people sign up at the end of the previous growing season (late fall). (I send in my check for the coming year's growing season before Christmas.) Some CSA farms expect that you'll pay to join *and* volunteer as part of your membership. That's the deal at the CSA farm I join each year. I am required to give eight hours of my time to help out at some point during the growing season. Last summer I did everything from weeding the green-bean fields to trimming garlic bunches. I also spent one hot and sweaty morning in the loft of a barn separating rotting onions from fresh ones.

In addition to the designated produce that is yours to take home each week, most CSA farms have pick-your-own fields that you can peruse as well. Last year we were able to get our fill of herbs, such as basil, thyme, and oregano, and freshly cut flowers when they were in bloom. My daughters always enjoyed going to the pick-your-own berry fields, where they usually ate their weight in blackberries or raspberries before we even got back to the car. And all of that extra pick-your-own items didn't cost a dime—those "privileges" were part of the subscription price we'd paid up-front.

Shopping for School Supplies

Recession or not, you've got to get your kids supplies when they go back to school. There's no getting around that. However, we frugal parents would like to get the most bang for our back-to-school buck without busting our budgets. Here are some ways you can do that.

It's Okay to Use Used Items

I'm guessing that with the popularity today of thrift and consignment shops, there is less stigma when you buy items used. I'm sure shopping on eBay has helped as well. Lucky for you, there are also ways that you can outfit your kid for school with gently used items.

For example, if your child needs a musical instrument for school lessons and you'd like to avoid the expensive cost of "leasing" an instrument, here are some more frugal options:

- Look for a used one on eBay or get it from a used-equipment store such as Music Go Round (*www.musicgoround.com*).
- Ask neighbors, family, and friends to see if they have any instruments they could lend to you or simply hand on down to your kid.
- Try local yard sales, log onto Craigslist, or fire up a "Wanted" message on a Freecycle list to see if anyone can help you out.

Invest in Products with Lifetime Guarantees

This may seem like the antithesis of frugal, but stick with me: it's worth it to spend a little bit more money on an item that is well-made, will last a long time, and/or comes with a lifetime guarantee. That's because once you buy something from a company that stands behind its products, you'll never have to pay for another one again—thus making your money, and your savings, go a longer way. Remember my winter coat anecdote from the introduction? That's what I'm talking about.

In addition to L.L. Bean, I know that Lands' End offers a lifetime guarantee on its products. So does Jansport, maker of backpacks and bags. Recently, Sears reintroduced its Kidvantage "Wear Out Warranty" program. It promises to repair or replace clothing or shoes that wear out before a child grows out of them.

Thanks to L.L. Bean's guarantee, I haven't had to buy a new backpack since my kids first started kindergarten. If anything did happen to one of their backpacks or I needed to replace a worn-out old backpack, I could return it to L.L. Bean for a newer model for free.

Take Advantage of Penny Deals

Even before school-supply lists show up in your mailbox over the summer, you should take advantage of penny sales to stock up on what you know your kids can always use more of—things such as Number Two pencils and two-pocket folders. Most national office supply chains and "big box" stores will run penny sales at some point during the year. Some of these penny sales let you buy one item at regular price and get a second one for just a penny. Other penny sales are exactly what they sound like—you get an item, with no strings attached, for anywhere from one to five cents. This is when you should be buying new school supplies rather than waiting for back-to-school shopping season, when you'll pay full price.

Shop at Home Before You Hit the Stores

When I say shop at home, I'm not talking about going online and buying stuff off of store websites. What I'm suggesting is this: look around your own home and see what kinds of extras or overruns you might have on hand that you can use to fulfill your kids' school supply requirements.

For example, a few years ago I started a school-supply box —a box in a closet that contains all kinds of school supplies. Everything in the box falls into one of two categories:

1. School supplies that I stocked up on when they were ridiculously cheap at the store, such as during the aforementioned penny sales.
2. School supplies that are leftover from previous years—either unused or so barely touched during the school year that I know my kids can use them again in coming school years. Besides three-ringed binders that still look new, items in this category include stretchy book covers, which I inspect at the end of the school year for pulls or tears. Then, if they look okay, I wash and dry them and put them back in the school supply box for the kids to use next year. I've got about six of those covers in rotation at any given time. At five bucks a pop, not having to buy six new covers at the beginning of each school year saves me $30 a year.

So when you have a school-supply box like I do, you really can shop at home for school supplies before you hit the stores. Since implementing our own supply box, we've slashed our school-supplies shopping bill from about $200 a year to about $50.

Don't Forget about Rewards Programs

Whenever possible, I sign up for a store's rewards program. With my CVS Extra Care card (*www.cvs.com*), I get coupons printed right on my receipt that I can use to save money on future purchases. With one of my store-affiliated credit cards, I earn points toward gift cards that help me get free groceries. And at Staples, which is the nearest office-supply store to me, I'm a member of the Staples Rewards (*www.staples.com*) program.

At least twice a year, I get a Staples rewards check, which I can cash in when I shop there. I try to save these rewards checks for when I need to buy school supplies. This way, I can sometimes manage to get out of the store, school supplies in hand, and not spend a dime out of my own wallet.

Total Savings in This Chapter

I guarantee that, having read this chapter, you will never look at shopping the same way again. We covered lots of different ways you can save on clothing, groceries ($300 a month in addition to $200 a year on fruits and vegetables), and school supplies ($200 a year).

Possible savings in Chapter 2: $4,000 a year

chapter three

APPLIANCES THAT DON'T SUCK . . . ENERGY, THAT IS

Not every appliance I own is the most energy efficient. That would seem counterproductive, given our frugal ways. But I don't stress out too much over the fact that my refrigerator was built the year I started high school, or that our washer and dryer are older than my teen. I'm not blissfully ignorant about how much energy older appliances use. I've just figured out ways to transform how I use these appliances so that, for all intents and purposes, they are, in fact, energy efficient. This was an important thing for us to do, since, for example, kitchen appliances account for up to 20 percent of a household's energy bills.

Even though newer models may be more energy efficient, it's still more frugal to use the ones you have until they no longer work. When you do have to buy new appliances, you should, of course, shop for great deals and check for Energy Star ratings. But in the meantime, learn how to use what you have in more efficient ways.

That's why in this chapter I'm going to share my secrets to energy-saving success. I'll help you rethink how you use such everyday household appliances as the washing machine, refrigerator, dishwasher, and stove. You'll learn how you can minimize your electric costs while still enjoying the items you own and taking care of your family, too.

Washing Machine and Dryer

If your daily life is anything like mine, then you probably feel as if you've always got a load of laundry going, or as if there are always clean clothes sitting in a basket somewhere waiting to be folded and put away. Turns out my everyday-laundry feeling isn't too far from the truth: according to the Consumer Energy Center (part of the California Energy Commission), the average American household does 400 loads of laundry a year—or a little more than a load a day. No wonder I feel as if I live in the laundry room. Even if your washing machine is always running, you can learn to operate it more efficiently.

Wash Full Loads Only

It doesn't take very long for our clothes hamper to fill up enough that I have a full load of laundry. However, there are times when I'll have just a few items that need to be washed right away, and I'm tempted to switch my top-loading washing machine setting from "super" load to "small" load. But I don't. That's because I know that I will use less energy overall if I only run the washing machine for large loads. Because when you think about it, the washing machine is going to be running and using electricity for the same amount of time, regardless of the load size you're doing. So why not get the most laundry clean each time you turn on the washing machine?

Here's another reason to do large loads only: Washing full loads can save the average home 3,400 gallons of water each year, says appliance maker Electrolux. With the average per-gallon cost of utility-provided water at around $.004, I realize that only adds up to $13.60, but every little bit helps. And saving water is good for Mother Earth, but that's fodder for another book I can write in the future on green living, right?

Wash in Cold Water Only

Want to hear something amazing? When you wash your clothes in hot water, 90 percent of the energy you use is heating that water. If the average home spends between $400 and $600 each year heating water, then switching to cold-water washes can save you money big time. You know what else is amazing? Cold water can get your clothes as clean as (if not cleaner than) warm or hot water. And you never have to worry about the dreaded "pink" clothing that results when colors run together during a hot-water wash.

Run the Shortest Washing Cycles Possible

When you look at most washing machines, you'll see different settings based on the fabric or make of the clothing you're washing (cotton versus permanent press), or the state the laundry is in (for example, "heavy duty"). I'd always assumed that "heavy duty" would be the setting of choice for moms with little boys who like to play in the mud.

It doesn't matter how dirty the clothes in my house are—I wash everything on the light-to-medium cycle. How do I manage to get my super-soiled items clean without wasting my money? Here are some of my tricks:

- Pretreat all stains. If something is really dirty or my daughter has spilled ketchup on her shirt, I know better than to just throw the item in the washing machine and hope for the best. First, I scrape off as much of the staining matter as possible. Next, I'll wet the fabric on and around the stain to try to loosen it among the fabric's fibers. Then, I will pretreat the stain by making a paste of Borax and liquid laundry detergent such as Tide (or plain water if I have no liquid detergent on hand). I rub it in and then let the paste sit on the item overnight. The next day, I'll throw it in the regular laundry, and it usually comes out clean. If it doesn't, I'll repeat the steps above. I'll usually rinse, lather, and repeat three times, and if the stain doesn't come out, then I declare the item a rag.
- Let loads soak. If you read a washing machine manual, you'll discover a dirty little secret about those heavy-duty washing settings—they usually involve some sort of soak cycle. Well, why use all the energy on a heavy-duty setting when you can do the following instead: fill your washing machine, let it agitate for a few minutes, and then turn it off and let the clothes soak for free.

With my washing machine, switching to the "extra heavy" cycle involves more than fifteen minutes of washing *per cycle* (wash, rinse, and drain), for a total of forty-five minutes that the washing machine is using energy. This does not include the spin cycle. Rather than use all of that energy, I'll keep the cycle on medium-to-light (that's six to nine minutes of agitating per cycle), but I will let those heavily soiled loads soak overnight by turning the washing machine off.

With the clothes soaking for twelve hours or so, it's as good as using the heavy-duty cycle without using all of that energy. That means it's cheaper for me to do my laundry in the long run, even if it means a load can take a really long time to be done.

SEAL OF APPROVAL *FRONT-LOADING WASHING MACHINE*

If you're in the market for a new washing machine, consider a front-loading (or horizontal axis) washing machine over a traditional, top-loading kind. I had one of these washing machines in my old house, and it was heartbreaking having to leave it behind. Here's why I became such a huge fan of front loaders.

For starters, front loaders use about twenty to twenty-five gallons of water per load versus the forty gallons of water per load that top loaders use. Then there is overall energy usage. According to the Environmental Protection Agency, a front-loading washing machine consumes about half the energy of a top-loading washing machine. Finally, front-loading machines tend to be gentler on clothes when washing them. They spin more like a dryer, in that they "tumble" the clothes through the water as they clean them. The top loaders have an agitator in the center of the machine that is much rougher on clothes overall, meaning that clothes washed in a traditional top loader may wear out faster than those washed in a front loader.

Granted, front loaders cost more than top-loading washing machines. But given that they save money and energy, and they may make your clothes last longer overall, I'm confident you'll make your money back in the long run. That's why I'm giving my Suddenly Frugal Seal of Approval to front-loading washing machines.

Change How You Use the Dryer

Experts say that the lowly clothes dryer is a monster energy user. Next to the refrigerator, it is the biggest power sucker in the house. Some estimate that over the lifetime of this appliance, your dryer will have cost you $1,600 in energy costs (gas and/or electric, depending on what you have). That's nothing to sneeze at.

Unfortunately, energy-efficient dryers don't exist, so says the Consumer Energy Center. It doesn't matter what brand you buy or how fancy the label is—a dryer is a dryer is a dryer. Think about it this way: All dryers work the same way. They move clothes around in a heated environment in order to dry them.

However, you can put your dryer on an energy diet—and spend less running one—by trying some of these tricks.

- Run loads back to back. Most of the energy that the dryer uses is for heating up the metal drum inside. If you're able to dry batch after batch of laundry, without ever letting the dryer drum cool down, your clothes will dry faster and you won't spend as much on energy. This advice works well when you've got a lot of linens to launder and no clothesline for hanging them out to dry.
- Dry on the moisture-sensor setting. This concept is really quite simple: certain dryers have built-in sensors so they can tell when clothes are still wet and when they're not anymore. Then the dryer automatically adjusts the temperature and the length of the drying cycle based on the moisture it senses. According to Energy Star, these settings really do work and can cut down significantly on how long your dryer runs—and therefore how much energy it uses.
- Clean the lint trap before each use. A gunked-up lint trap cuts down on the air circulating through the dryer, meaning

that the dryer will have to run longer and work harder to dry your clothes. This can run up your energy bill when all you needed to do was clean out the dryer's lint trap.

Refrigerator

In a perfect world, I would replace my refrigerator tomorrow. That's because, as I mentioned earlier, refrigerators use more energy than any other appliance in the house. Plus, older fridges (like many older appliances) simply don't run as efficiently as newer ones. Case in point: our main refrigerator, which came with the house and was made in 1979, costs $117.98 a year in electricity to run. Okay, so that works out to a little less than $10 a month, which doesn't seem so bad. However, we also have an overflow refrigerator, which was made in 1999 and has a decent Energy Star Rating. We brought this fridge with us from our old house. How much does it cost in electricity to run each year? Just $39, or a little more than $3 a month.

Sure, I'd like to save $80 a year in energy costs, but a new, similarly sized refrigerator would cost close to $1,000. I'm not sure I can justify that expenditure right now, and perhaps you can't either. That's why I'd like to share with you some of the ways I've learned to make my inefficient appliances, such as the refrigerator, run as efficiently as possible.

Here are five things you can try:

1. Shut the door! Remember what your mother said about never leaving the fridge open unnecessarily? Well, as with so many things with moms, she was right that it wasted energy. You see, every time you open the refrigerator door, 30 percent of the cold air inside escapes. This means that

the refrigerator has to work even harder to cool everything down again. So when you stand there, door open, and you're undecided about what you want to eat, just imagine your electric bills getting bigger and bigger. Also, when the door stays open and the inside of the fridge warms up, you're upping your risks that your food will spoil faster. And then you'll just have to replace your perishables sooner than usual, which could throw your grocery bill out of whack.

2. Keep your refrigerator and freezer well stocked at all times. The more items there are inside both sections of this appliance, the more efficiently it runs. Just as an open door lets out the cold air, a full refrigerator has less space that it has to fill with cold air, meaning the motor has to run less often.
3. Clean the coils. Let me ask you something: when was the last time you cleaned out the coils in the back of your fridge? Dirty coils make a refrigerator run harder, thus using more electricity. It's kind of like the lint trap in your dryer. Granted, you don't have to clean the refrigerator coils daily or every time you use it, like the dryer, but at least twice a year, vacuum the dust off the coils.
4. Give your fridge some space. The inside of your refrigerator may be cold but the back of it can get very hot. That's why it's a good idea to make sure that there is some space between the back of the refrigerator and whatever it is that it backs up to. In other words, there should be a smidge of breathing room between the coils and the wall. In addition, you don't want the refrigerator to run hotter (on the outside) than it has to. So Energy Star recommends that you keep the sides and back of your refrigerator away from anything hot. This could be your oven, your dishwasher, or a sunny window.

5. Make a regular habit of checking to see that the refrigerator and freezer doors seal tight when they close. They should kind of "stick" when you shut them. If the door bounces back open when you close it, you need a new door seal. Another sign of a leaky seal is any condensation that builds up on the outside of the refrigerator or freezer. Yet another test: close a piece of paper in the door, and try to pull it out. If it comes out easily, your seal is fried. You should be able to order a new seal from the refrigerator's manufacturer and install it yourself. Don't try to fix the problem with the same kind of weather stripping you might use around an exterior door. It may cause more problems than it fixes with your fridge.

Stove and Oven

When it comes to your stove and oven, keeping them frugal is more about your cooking habits than the appliance itself. Cases in point:

- If you have an electric stove with coil burners, you should match the pot size to the size of the burner. Otherwise, you're wasting energy. According to Energy Star, a six-inch pot placed on an eight-inch burner uses only 60 percent of the surface area, meaning that 40 percent of the burner's heat goes to waste.
- Cover your stovetop pots. This helps keep the heat inside and makes food cook faster. And as you know, if something can cook faster, then you get to turn the stove off sooner.
- Keep the oven door shut. With regard to the oven, don't keep opening the door to check on your food's progress. Just as

keeping a refrigerator door open lets the cold air escape, with an oven the same thing happens with heat. And the more hot air that gets out, the longer you'll need to keep the food in the oven. This is why most ovens have glass in the door and a switch that turns a light on inside so you can check your progress without messing with your cooking time.

Countertop and Smaller Appliances

Here's the good news about all those countertop and smaller appliances you may have in your kitchen—the microwave, coffeemaker, toaster, mixer, and more. They use very little energy when they are plugged in and turned on. And since they're not on for hours at a time, you shouldn't stress about how they may be stressing your electricity budget. Note: as with other plugged-in appliances that draw energy even when they're turned "off," you should keep all of your unused countertop appliances unplugged when you're not using them. I do splurge and keep my microwave plugged in, because I like having that clock as a reference. Plus, I did some research and discovered that my plugged-in microwave uses about $4 worth of energy a year when not in use. Now if I had twenty other plugged-in, unused appliances drawing the same amount of energy, I might draw the line at the microwave. But for right now, it makes more sense in my lifestyle not to have to reset the microwave every morning and, instead, keep it plugged in 24/7.

Microwaves

One thing to keep in mind when cooking meals: your microwave uses the least amount of cooking energy in your kitchen. Also, when it's warm out and you want to steam vegetables, doing so in the microwave (as opposed to the stovetop) helps to keep your kitchen cool. Here's another bonus for cooking veggies in the microwave: they retain more nutrients than vegetables cooked on the stove. Why? Some experts believe it's because microwave ovens use less heat and shorter cooking times than stoves.

Learn from a Slow Cookin' Woman

If you're interested in figuring out ways to use your slow cooker for more meals, check out the blog "A Year of Slow Cooking" (*http://crockpot365.blogspot.com*). This blog grew out of one mom's quest to make 365 days of dinners using only her Crock-Pot. Not only did the woman behind the blog, Stephanie O'Dea, meet her goal—and introduce me to some awesome, inexpensive recipes that I've since made for my family—but she got a book deal, too. Look for her book *Make It Fast, Cook It Slow: The Big Book of Everyday Slow Cooking* (Hyperion, 2009).

Slow Cookers

Your next best cooking option, as far as energy is concerned, is your Crock-Pot or slow cooker. Though you usually turn this appliance on for six to eight hours at a time, it uses so little energy to cook an entire meal that if you're looking to spend less on energy when cooking meals, you might want to consider using your slow cooker more often. For example, a meal in a slow cooker, simmering away for seven hours on low, will use only about 75 watts of electricity on low or 150 watts on high for the entire cooking period. A microwave oven uses about 1,500 watts of energy per hour (but who keeps a microwave on for an hour?) whereas a conventional oven burns through 2,000 watts *per hour* when in use. Imagine how much energy it takes to cook that Thanksgiving turkey.

Dishwasher

I'll bet you would think that washing dishes by hand would be the frugal way to get your dishes clean. Well, guess what? You would be wrong. An automatic dishwasher will always end up using less water to clean a full load than if you washed those dirty dishes by hand, meaning you won't boost your water bill in the process.

Some of today's newer, more efficient dishwashers use as little as five gallons of water for the entire dishwasher load. On the other hand, says the American Water Works Association, when you wash dishes by hand, the average person uses twenty gallons of water.

Where you can find some additional savings with your dishwasher is in the drying cycle. That is, don't use it all the time. When the dishwasher is done with its final rinse cycle and clicks over to the drying cycle, turn it off. Open the door, gently shake each rack to get the extra water off the dishes, then pull the racks out to full extension and leave them this way to dry. Not only will you save energy and electricity by not using the drying cycle, but also in the dry winter months, you'll have added some much needed (and free) moisture to the atmosphere in your house.

If dripping wet dishes freak you out and you'd like the dishes to dry all together inside the dishwasher, then at least use the air-dry setting. Choosing that setting over heated drying every time you run the dishwasher will save $12 a week in energy costs—or $624 a year—assuming you run the dishwasher once a day. I sometimes end up running the dishwasher in the morning and then again at night. In households like mine, just think about how much money I'm saving by skipping the drying cycle.

Water Heater

If you've read this far, then you're starting to understand that heating water can be a big part of what you're paying for when you pay your energy bill. Just recall the stat from earlier in this chapter in the washing machine section—90 percent of the energy used to run the washing machine is spent heating the water. Cut out the hot-water wash loads and you'll save yourself a bundle.

But what to do about the rest of the times when you need hot water? Well, if you have on-demand hot water or a heat pump, those are already pretty efficient ways of getting hot water into your house. So it's really just those houses with traditional water heater tanks that may be able to take some steps to reduce their energy use and therefore save money on hot water. If that describes your home, here are ways you can save money on hot water:

- Lower the water temperature on your water heater from the standard 140 degrees to 120 degrees. Doing so can save you up to 10 percent on your heating costs, or $60 a year.
- Install water-saving showerheads and aerators on sinks and faucets. These devices slow down the delivery of water, which, if you like long showers, can cut down on the amount of hot water you use. They can save you money as well. According to the experts at Lowe's, one low-flow showerhead can shave $65 off your annual water bill.

- Instruct everyone in the family to opt for showers over baths. Do that and you'll save forty gallons of water per shower.

Improve the Insulation Around the Water Tank

If you put your hand near your water tank and you can feel heat coming off it, heat is escaping from it. Then the tank must work harder to stay warm. Wrap the tank in insulation or a special thermal blanket that is safe for water heaters to cut down on this heat loss. Ask an expert at a home improvement store for recommendations on this kind of insulation or thermal blanket. Don't just throw Aunt Bessie's crocheted blanket around the water heater and secure it with a bungee cord. This is not only inefficient but it could be dangerous, too, since the blanket might catch fire—especially if you have a gas-fired water heater where there is usually an exposed flame at the bottom of the tank.

Be Ready for Your Next Water Heater Purchase

Most water heaters only have a life expectancy of between ten and twenty years. If yours is nearing its retirement age, visit the Energy Star website (*www.energystar.gov*) to research replacement options. Though it will cost you money up-front to replace your water heater, those water heaters that are older than ten years are practically dinosaurs—and it's a miracle that they're still working. Because they are running at half the efficiency of newer water heaters, spending now on a new one should save you money down the line.

Also, when you are considering getting a new water heater, think about changing the kind of water-heating system that you have. There are new tax credits available for people who purchase Energy Star–rated water heaters. In 2009 and 2010 only, if you purchase a non-solar water heater, you can get a tax credit of as much as 30 percent, up to $1,500. Considering that the average water heater costs about $800, you could be looking at a $240 tax credit.

As far as solar water heaters go, the government will also give you a 30 percent tax credit, with no upper limit on how much that 30 percent adds up to, and this tax credit is good through 2016. Some states offer additional tax credits for these purchases. Search the Energy Star website for "water heater tax credit" for more information.

Use a Dehumidifier to Get Free Water

Speaking of water, I wanted to share with you how my dehumidifier, which I run in the summer to help keep my house cool, has become a free source of water for me. Here are some of the ways I use that free water to save money on my water bill overall.

- Pour it into the washing machine as I'm filling a load. I figure that if the dehumidifier water helps to fill up the washing machine's tub, the washing machine itself will use less water in that first cycle.
- Use it to flush the toilets. The force of the water being dumped "flushes" the toilet without my having to touch the handle.
- Fill the kitchen sink with the water to let dirty dishes soak. Dehumidifier water isn't potable so I can't refill the dog's water dish with it. But I can use it to soak off stuck-on gunk on dishes before placing them in the dishwasher.

- Dump it in our swimming pool. Of course, this option will stay viable for only as long as the pool stays open. But, then again, I tend not to run the dehumidifier during the cold weather months, because it isn't humid out. Nonetheless, on a regular basis throughout the summer, we need to refill the swimming pool, because water naturally evaporates over time. By dumping the dehumidifier's nearly four-gallon water receptacle once a day, it does add up so that I can run the hose less often when filling the pool, and still keep the water at an optimal level for swimming.

Total Savings in This Chapter

I think it's interesting that a lot of the savings advice I've offered in this chapter could be construed as green or eco-friendly advice. And though that may be true, my mission in sharing these tips was to illustrate how making energy-saving changes in your house doesn't just save on carbon emissions—it saves money, too. Using less water when you wash clothes and washing only in cold water can bring you savings of more than $600 annually. If you lower your water heater's thermostat by 20 degrees, and avoid the heated drying setting on your dishwasher, you've just added another $60 and $624 in annual savings, respectively. Install a low-flow showerhead in one bathroom, and you'll shave $65 per year off your water bills. And if you're in the market for a new water heater, buying an average-priced Energy Star-approved model provides a $240 tax credit.

Possible savings in Chapter 3:
$1,360 a year

plus the one-time $240 tax credit

chapter four

ROOMS FOR IMPROVEMENT

How much time, imagination, and kilowatts are kids wasting every day at home? The modern playroom is chock full of time-suckers and energy-wasters, and it all probably costs a pretty penny. This chapter helps parents help their kids to streamline their toys and sell the excess to make extra cash, and teaches you how to reduce energy consumption with twenty-first-century game choices, such as gaming systems, computers, and other plugged-in entertainment.

In addition, most families likely think of their basement and garage as just space to store stuff, but these spaces can wreak havoc on utility bills. This chapter will show you how to rethink the way you use your garage and basement, why better insulation makes sense, and how the use of dehumidifiers can cut cooling costs.

Playroom

Sometimes when I walk in to my kids' playroom, I feel as if all the reminders of our past spendthrift ways are there to taunt me. If you were to look at the shelves, bins, and closets full of entertainment that my kids have, you would think we were running a retail business. It's like I had ten kids, not two. We may have gotten more frugal in lots of areas of our lives in the past few years, but in the playroom there was still a lot of work to be done. Not only were we seriously behind in thinning out the kids' entertainment but it was high time to do an energy audit of all the electronics that were eating up electricity 24/7, even though the kids were only in the playroom for a few hours a day.

Saving Energy

One of the first things we did when we decided to do this energy audit was to relocate all the electronics in the room into one area. After moving everything into that designated spot (which happens to be a large TV cabinet), we plugged the TV, DVD player, and various gaming systems into a single power strip.

I like having everything plugged in this way. Why? Well, when the kids are in that room watching TV or playing video games, it's easier for them to know where and how to turn their various electronics on. And then, when they're done with their fun, it allows them to turn everything off (thus stopping the energy suck) in one fell swoop—or one push of a button on the power strip. The only caveat to this setup was our TiVo: we needed it plugged into its own separate power source since it had to be turned on all the time to record shows around the clock (but the TV can stay off).

Here's another energy-saving tip for the playroom: when the room isn't in use, shut off its heating or air conditioning supply.

I mean this quite literally. If your playroom is on a separate thermostat from the rest of the house, as ours is, or even if the playroom is on the same heating-and-cooling grid as the rest of the house, you can close any vents into the room, shutter the windows or close the blinds, and then keep the door shut. You'll use less energy (and spend less money) heating or cooling your entire house by keeping only the rooms you're currently using open.

Decluttering to Bring in Cash

Once you have all your playroom electronics in one place, you can start taking inventory of what you own, what you want to keep, and what you might be able to clear out, just to declutter—or perhaps to get some cash in the process. We had reason to do this kind of inventory this past Christmas, after we'd surprised our daughters with a Wii. We needed to make room in our electronics cabinet for this new gaming system, and while we were at it, we decided to organize all the games in the playroom—from Xbox and PlayStation (yes, we have both) to board games and more. We also decided to re-evaluate the furniture in the room to ensure that the playroom wasn't just a crowded room with wall-to-wall stuff but rather a room where we could all enjoy playing games together.

Here's how we met our decluttering goal: We pretty much took every piece of furniture, box of videos, and stack of board games out of the room. Literally—we piled everything in the hall. Then, one by one, we put things back in—but only if we thought we would use it. In the process we matched up game controllers with their respective gaming systems—previously, they were spreading like vines around the edges of the playroom floor—and returned all of the homeless DVDs to their cases.

We also discovered a lot of items that did not need to go back into the playroom. These were games that my kids had outgrown, movies they weren't interested in watching for the 101st time, and videotapes that just didn't have the same allure as shiny DVDs. In addition, we realized that one of the couches in the playroom had seen better days. Though the kids didn't care about its state of being, we figured that if we could move the couch elsewhere, we could really open up the playroom to make it more livable.

By the end of the day, we ended up with three huge bins of VHS videos that my kids had outgrown. I sold them on eBay and made about $50 in the process. In addition, we decided to sell that worn-out couch. Thanks to a Craigslist ad, a college student gave us $30 for it. He told us it was perfect for his fraternity house.

Some of the games and movies we weren't quite sure what to do with; we decided to put them away in the basement. Then, when the kids grow bored with the games and movies currently in rotation, we can pretend it's Christmas morning and bring out those old games and movies as if they're brand new. I've heard from plenty of parents who follow this toys-and-games-in-rotation approach to keep their playrooms clutter free and to keep their kids from growing bored too quickly with their games, toys, and entertainment.

Finally, if you do notice that your kids have outgrown some toys, even when they're "new" into rotation, encourage your kids to get rid of them on their own and maybe make a little money in the process. You might be surprised to discover at what a young age a child can show her entrepreneurial tendencies.

When my own daughters were eight and ten, I suggested that they start selling some of their tried-and-tired toys on eBay or Craigslist as a way of making some extra cash. With a little help from me, they put together mixed lots of Polly Pocket, Barbie, and Bratz dolls, took pictures of their lots, and then uploaded their descriptions for what they were selling to these websites. Time and time again, my daughters were able to make anywhere from $30 to $80 on toys they might have just thrown away. This was money they could use to supplement their allowance or put in the bank for college.

Basement

In some homes the playroom may actually be in the basement, so there's no reason for me to repeat any of the advice I've just offered. However, basements are also an area of the house where you can experience a lot of energy loss or waste, just by the very nature of the space. This is where the frugal-minded need to step up their preventive measures so that they can save money down the road.

For example, is part of your basement unfinished? If so, this unfinished part is likely sucking away all of the hot or cold air that you're using to keep the rest of your basement temperate. That's why it's important to have a barrier—a physical barrier—between the finished and unfinished part of the basement. In most instances a new wall with a door is all you need. But maybe you don't have the time or the resources to put up a wall or a door. That's okay. Even draping a sheet or blanket across the opening between the two rooms can cut down on heating and cooling loss.

Here's something else you'll likely find in your basement—your water heater. In Chapter 7, "The Warm and Cold of It," I discuss the notion of saving money on heating and cooling, and in the previous chapter, I'd talked about making your water heater as efficient as possible. It bears repeating that if you have a water heater or hot-water pipes that are in an unfinished portion of your basement, it might make sense to wrap them in some kind of insulation. That way any heat they generate isn't lost to the unheated area in which they sit.

What about your power and light source in your basement? I know that most houses I've lived in have had a light switch at the top of the basement stairs. When you flip it on, that switch turns on all of the lights in the basement—even if you're only going into one room. To save energy and save money, why not do what my mother, the original frugalista, does in her basement? She has arranged it so that only two lights go on when she switches the lights on at the top of the basement steps. How did she arrange this? By removing the light bulbs from the ceiling light fixtures in the basement that came with the house. If she needs additional light when she's down there, she has placed other, freestanding lights that she must manually switch on and off. Oh, and it goes without saying that all of these lights have compact fluorescent bulbs in them, not traditional light bulbs, so they use as little energy—and run up as small an electricity bill—as possible.

Heating and Cooling

Here's another energy-saver for the basement: control the humidity level so you'll spend less when heating and cooling the basement. As I mention in Chapter 7, the humidity level in your house can work to your benefit or against it. In other words, during the winter if you can raise the humidity of the air inside, it will feel warmer without your having to turn up the heat. Conversely, in the summer if you run a dehumidifier so that the humidity level stays low, your home will feel cooler without your having to crank the air conditioner.

If your laundry room happens to be in the basement, you can immediately increase the humidity level during winter by hanging your wet clothes up to dry. In our old house, we strung a clothesline through the length of the basement, and I hung up everything as if I were drying my laundry outside. Come summer, I just made sure to keep our dehumidifier running, which helped my clothes dry quickly as well as keeping the air in the basement cool without any air conditioning on at all.

And it goes without saying that if you do have heating or cooling vents in your basement, it's a good idea to close them off—as you would turn out the lights—when no one is using the basement. Why spend money heating or cooling a space that no one is in?

Storage Solutions

Though I mentioned that I'll take toys out of rotation from the playroom and put them in the basement for use at a later date, the key to using your basement (or garage) for storage and remaining true to your frugal mission is making sure you keep things in an organized fashion. The worst thing you could do is to stock up on tools, toys, or trinkets that you think you'll need some time in the future, only to lose them in a mess of clutter. How many times have you searched for something you need—say, a screwdriver—and when you couldn't find it where it was supposed to be, you went out and bought a new one? And then what happened? After you got the new screwdriver home and maybe used it a few times, you found your old one. Now you have two screwdrivers, which probably isn't the worst thing in the world, but the fact that you spent money on something unnecessarily isn't great either.

If your basement or garage looks like mine used to, then it's piled to the rafters with "someday I might need this" stuff. Well, you know what? It's time to change things up. Here's what you need to do. You need to take a couple of weekends and go through your "someday" stuff, and determine one of three things about this stuff.

1. You definitely will need or use this in the future, so now you need to store it in a well-labeled container that's easy to reach.
2. You don't think that you're ever going to use those twenty grass skirts that you got on sale at the party supply store (or whatever you discover that has you saying "What was I thinking when I bought this stuff?"). Therefore, you need to put them in a container that you'll bring upstairs to sell on eBay or Craigslist, give away on Freecycle, or donate to a good cause.
3. You know you're never going to need this stuff and, frankly, it's all junk anyway. (This time you might be saying to yourself, "What was I thinking holding on to this crap?") Get a big garbage bag or empty box to toss the worthless items in, drag it out to the street, and then put a "curb alert" message on Freecycle. For anything that might be recyclable, drag down your recycling container, and put that out on your next recycling pickup day. The idea is to clear out the basement, and not to continue to store this junk to deal with on some future day.

Finally, if you find you have the space to do this in the basement, you might want to create an overflow pantry for canned goods and other food that you stock up on at the grocery store when they're on sale. If the conditions are right, you might also be able to turn a portion of your basement into a root cellar. This is where you can store apples, onions, potatoes, winter squash, turnips, and other root vegetables after a late fall harvest. When you have a place to store these fruits and vegetables, you can take advantage of low prices when these fruits and vegetables are in season, and save yourself a lot of money by having your own stash of (relatively) fresh produce that you can dip into over the cold winter months.

Most experts agree that ideal conditions for a root cellar are a space that's between forty and fifty degrees consistently. So an unfinished portion of a basement may be your best bet. If you're serious about giving a root cellar a try, contact your state's land-grant university or co-op extension program—the folks that focus on agriculture, basically—and see if they can give you a quick course in root cellars 101.

Garage

You may just see your garage as a place to store your cars—and your garbage pails, the lawnmower, and whatever else you can fit in around its perimeter. But a well-used garage can also help you along the path to frugality, both with how you use the garage and with what you store in it.

Car Talk

Let's start with your car. Did you know that a car that you keep in the garage will last longer than one parked outside? That's because nature's elements can contribute to your car's breakdown over time. This is especially true if you live near the ocean—salt water is a car's worst enemy and contributes to rusting like nobody's business. Bright sunshine also contributes to rust, because it speeds up oxidation of the metal. To you and me, that means that a car that is always sitting outside in the sun will rust faster, even if there's no water present.

Here's another way parking your car in the garage can help save you money: when it's cold and snowy out, you don't have to run the car to defrost the windows or warm it up. In the summertime, you won't have to run the air conditioner at full blast to cool down a hot car either.

If you don't have a garage, then at least put your car inside a carport, under a cover, or beneath some shady trees. It's better than letting it bake outside in the sun.

Heating and Cooling

Did you know that your attached garage may be adversely affecting how much you use the heat or air conditioner on any given day? This is especially true if you haven't insulated your garage, you leave the big garage door open, or you don't have an insulated door that leads into the house.

Another way the door between the house and garage can increase your heating and cooling bills is if it's letting in drafts, or you find yourself opening and closing it a lot, such as to let pets in or out. If your dog or cat gets outside via the inside garage door, consider installing a pet door instead on that door as well as the one that leads to the outside. If you find that the door leading into the house is drafty, you may have to adjust the doorknob catch so that the door closes tightly and/or install weather stripping so cold or hot air doesn't escape.

Overflow Refrigerator

Your garage could be unwittingly contributing to your higher energy bills if you keep an extra refrigerator in there. That's what we did in our old house, and the garage was probably the worst place we could have put that overflow refrigerator—even an energy-efficient one. We discovered after the fact that when a refrigerator is running in a space without insulation, it has to work twice as hard to maintain its internal temperature. In addition, when it is cold outside, if the temperature inside your garage drops below the temperature that the refrigerator is set to maintain (something around thirty-five degrees Fahrenheit), then the refrigerator will simply shut off and not try to get any cooler. This may explain why any ice cream we stored in that freezer during the winter was always soupy.

Home Office Equipment

In my home office, I have one surge protector/power strip. Currently, the following is plugged into it: laser printer, scanner, desktop computer, laptop computer charger, backup hard drive, and desk lamps. When I'm in the office and using everything, everything is on. But at night, I've gotten into the habit of shutting down all of the electronics—you know, powering them down—and then I take the extra step of flipping the switch on the power strip to turn it off as well. In using this power strip to turn my equipment off, I'm helping to save about 10 percent annually on my electric bills. Since my electric bills range from $150 to $300 a month, depending on the season, imagine how much more I'd be spending if I were leaving those electronics on all the time?

Speaking of leaving electronics on all the time, some people seem to believe that it's better to leave a computer on overnight, in sleep mode, than to shut it down and boot it up in the morning. These folks think that the extra energy burst you get when you turn a computer on negates any energy savings you might achieve from having the computer turned off overnight.

Here's the deal. True, there is a brief energy surge when you turn on a desktop computer. However, it doesn't even come close to the amount of energy an all-night computer is sucking from your home.

Besides saving money on energy bills, here's another reason to shut down your computer on a regular basis: it will last longer.

It seems that most computers are designed to have a finite life span, based on the hours they're used. So the longer you keep your computer turned on, even in sleep mode, the quicker you'll be on the road to a new computer. And though prices for computers have come way down in recent years, why add "buying a new computer" to your budget when by simply shutting the computer off regularly you could be putting off that purchase for months if not years?

Here are additional energy-saving tips as they relate to a home office from the U.S. Department of Energy's Office of Energy Efficiency and Renewable Energy (*www.eere.energy.gov*):

- Turn off a computer's monitor if you're going to be away from your desk for twenty minutes or more, and shut down the entire computer ensemble if you'll be out of the office for more than two hours.
- Keep your computer's sleep mode active no matter what. Having a computer switch into sleep mode when it's idle can cut down on its energy use by up to 70 percent.
- Don't rely on screen savers as your "sleep" mode. A screen saver bouncing across your computer screen actually eats up just as much energy as when you're actively using your computer.

Recycle Home-Office Equipment for Cash

The closet of our home office is like a mausoleum for old equipment. It's where our old printers go to die. We have so many printers in there because for a few years running, whenever we bought a new computer, we got a printer for free. And it wasn't as if you could refuse to take the printer and get additional money off on your computer purchase.

We also started collecting obsolete printers when we switched from using personal computers to Apple computers only, and then technology advanced to a point where the USB connector became the universal port. Suddenly we had a bunch of older printers that used serial cables, and we had no computers to attach them to anymore.

I try to bring those old printers with me each year when my county holds its household hazardous waste collection event, because then I know that at least the printers are being disposed of responsibly. But I'm thinking that from here on in, I'm going to try to bring in a little extra cash when I get rid of electronics.

Of course, I can try to sell them on Craigslist and maybe make a few bucks. But more likely I'm going to take advantage of companies that will recycle your electronics for you and give you cash for them. I'm thinking of Radio Shack's "trade in" program that started in 2008. You earn gift cards to Radio Shack based on exactly what kinds of electronics you trade in with them. (Check out the store's website at *www.radioshack.com/tradein* to find out the program's details.)

If you're an Apple customer and in the market for a new computer, you can often get some kind of credit to apply to a new purchase when you recycle your old Apple item through the company. For example, I know that last fall Apple would recycle your old iPod and give you 10 percent off a new iPod. So people who were planning to buy their kids an iPod for Christmas were able to get their shopping done early and get their kids the technology they wanted, plus they saved money in the process.

Even if you're not recycling old equipment, you should be recycling your print cartridges on a regular basis for the financial incentives they bring. Many office supply stores will give you a coupon off the purchase of your next print cartridge if you bring the used one into the store to be recycled. For a long time running,

I got a $3-off coupon from Staples every time I brought my used ink cartridges in with me when I bought new ink cartridges. Since I replace my cartridges four times a year, this gives me $12 back in my pocket for supplies I was going to buy anyway.

SEAL OF APPROVAL *POWER STRIPS*

As with other electronics in our home, we've started using a power strip for all of the chargers we need for our handheld electronics and gadgets. We call it our charging station, and it's where we keep the power cords for our laptops, cell phones, and digital cameras plugged in on any given day. Then, when nothing needs to be charged, we turn that power strip off.

There's no need to spend big bucks on these so-called "smart" power strips. They all work the same anyway. You plug your electronics into this one power source, and then when you're done, you flip the switch to turn everything off. Some experts estimate that you can save up to $200 a year in energy costs by using a power strip. Now that's a great way to keep our electricity costs in check, and the reason I'm giving a Suddenly Frugal Seal of Approval to power strips.

Total Savings in This Chapter

I'm amazed at how certain rooms in a house seem to hold unrealized money-making opportunities—from selling used toys in a playroom to getting money back when you recycle ink cartridges in the home office to saving money on your energy bills by using power strips.

Possible savings in Chapter 4: >$200 a year

chapter five

MIXING MEDIA WITH FRUGALITY

Just because a family decides to live a frugal life doesn't mean that they have to move in under a rock and never go out for fun. There are a number of ways to keep a family entertained without spending excess cash. This chapter gives you a ton of options for keeping up-to-date on the latest movies and books, and any other entertainment that you probably didn't think you could enjoy on a frugal budget.

For example, once we decided to take a scalpel to our entertainment expenses, I thought I would go into shock when I no longer had HBO available every time I turned on the TV. But once I realized how much we were saving by getting rid of HBO, I was a lot more comfortable with the decision. Just cutting out HBO alone allowed us to avoid paying close to $400 a year for a channel we watched perhaps two nights a week.

Bottom line: you can still enjoy lots of different kinds of entertainment when you're living frugally. The trick is figuring out the creative ways to see the movies or read the books or listen to the music you want without spending a lot of money in the process.

Entertainment Tonight with TV and Movies

So many people I spoke to when researching this book or writing my blog shared a dirty little secret about their TV entertainment experiences—they don't have cable service yet they can watch all of the TV shows, movies, and cable series that they want. How? They've figured out a work-around plan that saves them from having to pay the nearly $100 a month that most cable or satellite TV packages cost.

Think about that. No cable equals $1,200 a year in savings! With that in mind, let me share with you some of these work-around solutions so you, too, can watch TV and movies without actually having to pay full price for a satellite or cable TV subscription.

Sign Up for Netflix

I know, I know, signing up for something that costs money may seem counterintuitive in a book about frugal living. But get this: Netflix, the through-the-mail video-subscription service, offers different levels of membership, some of which may fit your frugal budget, especially if you're a movie lover. The cheapest one, which allows you take out one DVD at a time, costs only $8 a month. If you watch and return two movies per week per month, you'll spend only $1 per movie. The trick to making Netflix work on a frugal budget is making sure that you (a) return DVDs in a timely way to maximize your monthly fee and (b) watch enough movies that the price per movie gets reduced over time to the $1 mark. (You can learn more about

Netflix on its website: *www.netflix.com.*) In my mind a Netflix subscription is a perfect compromise for the movie lover who has to see every year's Academy Award–nominated films, doesn't want to pay $10 or more per ticket to do so, and doesn't mind waiting for the movie to leave the theaters and become available on DVD.

Enjoy the Silver Screen with Redbox

Redbox is a DVD-rental service that you can find in more than 1,200 stores nationwide (mostly supermarkets). It's pretty much a vending machine for movies that costs only $1 per flick per night (plus tax). Each Redbox kiosk can hold up to 200 different movies. You can get DVD's through Redbox in two ways. You can choose your movie on the spot using a touch screen on the kiosk. You pay with a swipe of your credit or debit card. Or you can visit *www.redbox.com* to choose a DVD and then pick it up at the nearest Redbox location. (Even some McDonald's have these Redbox kiosks.)

Log on for Your Film Fix

Assuming you've kept your Internet connection alive, you'll be pleased to know that the computer is the new TV. More and more video content is showing up online these days, and not just illegally uploaded episodes of *Lost* on YouTube. Sure, you can download an episode of shows such as *Top Chef* at $1.99 a pop on iTunes, but why pay when you can get something for free—and legally? Hulu.com is one of my favorite new websites. It's a free site that lets you watch any TV shows that you've missed and would otherwise have to pay to catch up on. Originally, Hulu.com seemed to be for NBC shows only, but a recent visit to the site uncovered episodes of *The Family Guy* (FOX) and *Paula's Home Cooking* (Food Network), just to name a few. The catch is that you have to register for an account (no biggie) and that some popular shows only stay on the site for a week or so (bummer). But given that you're getting free TV content, with just a few minor inconveniences thrown in, I'd say that Hulu.com is definitely worth checking out. It also allows you to watch shows that aired very recently—something you can't do with services such as Netflix. Plus, if you've got a big computer monitor like mine—it's the same size as the TV we have in the master bedroom—watching free shows via your computer could be a similar experience to actually watching them on a regular TV.

Borrow from the Library

If you haven't been to your local library in a long time, you may be pleased to discover how much more you can get these days with a library card. Sure, there are all the free books, magazines, and newspapers you can read (see below), but many libraries also have extensive movie collections.

When my kids were really little, I would take them to the library to borrow their favorite movies that I was too cheap to buy in the store or borrow (for a fee) from the video store. As you know with kids, once they have a favorite, they want to watch it again and again—until suddenly they don't want to watch it anymore. And trust me, that change of heart can happen in a split second.

Given kids' finicky entertainment tastes, that's reason alone *not* to spend money buying TV shows or movies for them to own. Instead, save money by borrowing movies from the library. But borrower beware: DVDs and videos often have shorter lending times than books, and heftier fines if you return them late. A DVD that's just a couple of days overdue could end up costing you the same as one bought new in the store.

Use Rewards Cards to Get Discount Movie Tickets

If you're such a film fan that you can't wait for films to come out on DVD (and then get them for free from the library), you may think that there's no hope for you. But there is a way you can still go to the movies and see first-run movies at a discount. Not free, mind you, but at a discount.

Are you a member of a warehouse club such as Costco? If so, then your membership gets you access to super-saver movie tickets, which you buy in bulk. (At this writing you had to buy tickets five at a time.) The tickets come out to $7.50 each, which around here is what you'd pay for a matinee (another great cost saver if you just have to see the movie when it's fresh in the theaters). But the benefit of the super-saver movie tickets is that you can use them during prime time, too.

You can snag discount movie tickets another way, too, such as by using your Borders Rewards card. If you sign up for Borders Rewards Perks (*www.bordersrewardsperks.com*), you can buy movie tickets in bulk just as you can with your Costco card. On average this reduces the per-ticket cost to $8.50; if you request tickets for older movies, you can pay as little as $7.50 per ticket.

So while not super-frugal, if you've got to get your movie house fix, at least these options offer you a way to spend a little less than you would if you were paying full price for the movie tickets.

Get Free Programs and Movies Through Your Cable Company

If you're not quite ready to part with your cable service, you can at least enjoy all of its benefits so you maximize your entertainment dollar. For example, as Comcast digital customers we get their "On Demand" service. This allows us to rent newly released movies for only about $4, which is way cheaper than a theater ticket. But when we're feeling super-cheap, we can peruse the "free movies" section of On Demand, and enjoy flicks for zero bucks. Recently, we watched some oldies but goodies, such as *Dirty Dancing* and *You've Got Mail*.

Other TV providers offer this same kind of "on demand" service. Take Verizon's FiOS TV. It, too, has a video-on-demand library that not only lets you select free movies but also lets you find some of your favorite TV shows on demand.

By (Not Buy) the Book on a Budget

One of my resolutions when I started living more frugally was to stop buying books and start borrowing them from the library. This resolution hit home our first year of living frugally when my husband and I revisited our book purchases from the previous year, something we do annually in advance of having our taxes done. (We review our credit card spending to uncover any expenses that are tax-deductible and that we should include on our tax returns. Some of these expenses are books when, for example, I interview an author for a magazine article and want to read that person's book first.)

Anyway, that year I kept seeing purchases from my three weaknesses—Amazon.com, Barnes & Noble, and Borders. And on their own, none of these purchases seemed like much and many of them ended up as legitimate tax deductions. But when I decided to add up all of this spending, the number that was staring back at me was scary—in one year we'd spent close to $800 on books alone. That, my friend, surely would not fly in our newly frugal household. Yet I didn't want to deny my family or myself the pleasure of reading, or affect my ability to research any stories I might be writing. That's why we had to come up with a book Plan B.

Use Your Library

One of the first changes I made was starting to use the library again. It was easier than I thought.

Does your library offer an online service like mine does? This is how it works for me: When I read about a great book in a magazine or newspaper, or hear an author speaking on TV or the radio, and want to read his or her book, I can log on to my library's website and reserve the book. Sometimes the staff just has to pull the book off the shelf at the library around the corner and call me to come pick it up; other times they need to "order" the book from another branch, and it gets to me in a couple of days.

One of the reasons that I love this online-reservation option is that it allows me to "get" books the same way I used to when I was buying them off of Amazon or Barnes & Noble. I would hear about a book that piqued my interest, and I would log on to buy it. With the library system, I can go through the same motions and do it just as quickly so I don't forget about it—except I don't have to enter my credit card number to complete the transaction. I just click on the "reserve" button. Then I can expect a call or e-mail from the library when the book is ready for me to pick up.

If you'd like to use your library to find books you can keep, don't forget that many branches have book sales with donated hardcover books and paperbacks. Whenever I've browsed through these book sales, I've come across many titles that haven't even had their bindings cracked. This allows you to secure books at an I-can't-believe-it price, and you'll support a good cause—your local library.

There are many other ways to secure free or low-cost books beyond your public library. Here are some additional options for you to consider.

Yard and Garage Sales

Every yard or garage sale I've ever been to has had at least one box of books for sale. And being the reader that I am, I usually end up leaving with a minimum of one new title under my arm. I never spent more than twenty-five cents on my reading material. It's probably a no-brainer for you to think about getting other kinds of almost-free stuff at yard sales, so I hope you'll think about books the next time you're perusing someone's sale in a driveway or front yard on a weekend morning.

Thrift and Consignment Stores

You could have a field day finding cheap books in a thrift or consignment shop. In fact, there are two kinds of these stores where I know you'll do well.

- A thrift store in a college town. At the end of the academic year, lots of college students dump their books at a local thrift store (assuming they can't sell them and make back some of their money) rather than cart them home. My mom lives near a Goodwill in a college town, and the book stock there is always impressive.
- A consignment shop that targets a certain demographic. Here I'm thinking specifically of Plato's Closet (*www.platoscloset.com*). This is a national franchise of consignment stores geared specifically to the 'tween and teen market. While the store focuses on selling attire and accessories, there is a section of books, CDs, and DVDs. One of my daughters was able to pick up a couple of books she'd wanted to read (but

hadn't been able to get out of the library) for a couple of dollars.

Swapping with Friends and Neighbors

There are a couple of ways to handle book swaps with people you know. You can do a round-robin sort of thing, where you set a timeline for passing along a book from one person to another. Or you can just swap whenever someone is desperate for something good to read. When I used to work in an office, the book-loving employees designated a spot where people could leave books that they'd read and others could take them in turn. Maybe you've got a space in your workplace—a teacher's room or a hallway—where you can set up an informal book swap center.

The great thing about swapping is that it doesn't always have to involve people you know—try the Internet! Here are some sites to peruse:

- The "barter" or "free" section of Craigslist for book offerings—find some or post some yourself
- Swaptree.com
- BookMooch.com
- PaperBackSwap.com
- Zwaggle.com (for babies and children)
- Bookins.com

Most of these sites are free (some may have a small annual charge) and work in a book "karma" way. You have to be willing to give away a certain number of books on your own dime—that is, you'll send them to people who want the books—before you can earn enough credits to request that others send you books for free (on their dime). I know many bookworms who swear by these swapping sites. Many have gotten more than just paperback books, mind you. Some readers have secured books on tape (or DVD) and music CDs, too.

Freecycle

I'm always seeing "Offer" ads on Freecycle from people who are giving away books. Just like yard sales and thrift stores, there's no guarantee that these books will be in optimal condition. However, when you're on a budget, you should take whatever book-getting opportunity comes your way.

Become a Book Reviewer

If you're a book lover and an aspiring writer, why not approach your local newspaper about writing a book review column? Once you've got the gig, you can get yourself on publishers' mailing lists, and they'll start sending you review copies of books for free. Read what you want for your column, and pass along others to friends. (FYI, if you get a review gig and want more information on book publishers, check out Publisher's Marketplace at *www.publishersmarketplace.com*. Don't worry about the login stuff on the homepage. You don't have to pay to join the website to search its member database.)

Make the Most of Magazines

Many of the methods for getting your magazine fix for free (or on the cheap) are the same as with books.

- Namely, your local library should have a huge selection of current magazines—some of which you may be able to check out. In addition, at my library, there is always a stack of magazines for sale in the foyer, usually for something like twenty-five cents each. Yours may have a similar section.

- I recently discovered that Freecycle can be a great resource for magazines, too. Nearly every week I'll see offers for magazines (usually the "home" kind, such as *Cooking Light* or *Southern Living*). Since I'm a reader who wants to tear out articles or recipes I can try later, getting free magazines off of Freecycle (which I can mutilate as I please) makes much more sense than borrowing them from the library.
- Reading your magazines on the Internet is probably the cheapest way to get the information you're seeking without spending a dime. Plus, if you like recipes, you can just print them out as needed.
- Check out the well-stocked magazine and newspaper racks at bookstores, and settle for reading these periodicals for free while you're in the store. While a viable option, this is not my first choice. Why? Because I know my limits and my temptations. And though I may not buy a magazine when I can look through it for free, I'm more likely to splurge on a delicious and expensive snack whenever I'm in one of these bookstores. That means that if I spend $3 on a cup of coffee and $2 on a baked good, I'm not really saving money in the long run.
- Swap magazines with friends and family. Surely someone you know gets a magazine you're interested in! In exchange, you can offer your subscription copies to them.

Magazine Subscriptions

I'd rather not leave magazine reading to chance, and that's why I subscribe to a number of magazines. But of course, I do it frugally. Buying them one a time just doesn't make any financial sense. If you pay at the newsstand or the checkout counter, you pay through the nose. But if you pay ahead of time for a subscription, you can cut your annual magazine costs in half, if not more.

For example, my subscription to *People* magazine, while not cheap, costs $100; purchasing the fifty-one issues from the newsstand would cost about $192. The other benefit of being a subscriber? I get a code with each issue that allows me to access additional information from the magazine's website that nonsubscribers can't see. Here are some other methods for lowering subscription costs:

- Use airline miles. I'm always getting magazine and newspaper subscription offers in the mail, and last year we were able to subscribe to a handful of publications without spending a dime. One such subscription was to the *Wall Street Journal.* Normally, that daily paper's annual subscription costs $156. By using up airline miles, I got it for free.
- Find a fundraiser. I've also secured inexpensive magazine subscriptions through an annual magazine drive/fundraiser that my daughters' school runs.
- Wait it out. Here's a subscription trick my mother recently learned: when you start getting renewal notices for a magazine, ignore them. Keep ignoring them until your subscription has almost run out. Then you may begin receiving additional renewal notices with significantly reduced prices. Though this doesn't work with every magazine subscription, the next time you're tempted to renew early, hold off, and see if the prices drop.

SEAL OF APPROVAL *EXERCISE TV*

Before I had kids, I was a gym rat. Then my free time got filled up with parental duties, and going to the gym just didn't fit in with my busy life. So we invested in a treadmill, and I started relying on walking on it—and walking the dog—as my aerobic exercise.

Now, six years later, I'm looking to switch things up but without spending money on a gym membership. About the time I was looking to add something new to my workout, a friend of mine, who had been looking extremely fit, told me that she'd been doing *The Biggest Loser* workouts. I'd heard of the show, but didn't know they had exercise programs, too. Turns out I can get two different "The Biggest Loser" workouts for free from my cable provider. They are available via Exercise TV On Demand, one of Comcast's offerings. Granted, the programs I get this way are only twenty minutes long (on DVD they run for a full hour), but, man, do these workouts kick my butt. No wonder people lose so much weight on the show. The best part about Exercise TV is that I get to exercise when I want to, not based on a gym schedule, and I'm not spending any extra money to do so.

And, Exercise TV doesn't just have these two "The Biggest Loser" workouts on it. There are at least a dozen different workout categories available, and then at least two different exercise programs within each category. With Exercise TV, I never have to think about a joining a gym again. It's the ultimate frugal workout tool. That's why Exercise TV has my Suddenly Frugal Seal of Approval.

Total Savings in This Chapter

I'm sure that when you started reading this chapter, you had a hard time believing that you could enjoy your favorite media and still remain true to your frugal mission. From giving up premium cable channels ($400) to borrowing books from the library ($800) to subscribing to magazines rather than buying them on the newsstand ($248), you can save a bundle yet still feel totally connected to pop culture.

Possible savings in Chapter 5: $1,400 a year

chapter six

GETTING FROM POINT A TO POINT B

What a crazy few years it's been for car owners. We've seen gas prices skyrocket to levels we never thought we'd see in this lifetime, then plummet down to levels we never thought we'd see again in this lifetime. I mean, if the roller coaster of the stock market isn't making you sick to your stomach from all of the lurches up and down, then gas prices might be.

Then there's this whole issue of car prices and gas mileage, and all the other pros and cons you have to consider when buying or leasing a car. With many automakers in trouble because people aren't buying cars, prices on the new- and used-car lots have been varying as much as those at the gas pump. Plus, with our country in a credit crunch, even if you wanted to buy a new car, you might not be able to secure the credit necessary to get a car loan.

So all told, this is either very good news for you as far as a new car goes or very bad news. But you know what? When it comes to living frugally, everything doesn't have to be black and white—even with regard to your car. The important thing is making an educated decision about what to buy and when.

Even if your family ends up keeping its SUV or monster car, there are ways you can travel from Point A to Point B without spending too much. That is, you can make a gas-guzzler into a gas sipper, just by changing your driving habits. In addition, if you really are in the market for a new car—if your old one is on the verge of breaking down—I'll help you figure out the pros and cons of certain car purchases or leases so that you can get around without depleting your bank account.

The Right Car for You

Let me tell you a little about our recent car-buying experience. I realize it may not match exactly with your needs, but how we approached our car purchases may help you in the long run. Basically, what has qualified as "the right car for us" has changed over time. When we were first married, we needed a get-around-town car that allowed my husband to drive to his job. For that, we bought a used Ford Escort hatchback. When we had kids, we upgraded (kind of) to a Ford Escort wagon so we had room for car seats and a stroller. Eventually we traded up again, to a minivan when carpooling to kids' activities became a part of our daily life.

When that minivan started limping along on its last legs, we had to decide on two things: Did it make financial sense to try and fix the minivan? And if not, what did the "right car for us" notion mean at that point?

Because the Kelley Blue Book value of that van was less than the $1,500 it would cost to repair the car's transmission, trading it in was the fiscally responsible thing for us to do. Now we just needed to figure out which automobile we should buy.

We went through our lifestyle and financial checklist to ensure we made the best decision possible. Here are some of the things we asked ourselves—and you should, too, when you find yourself needing to buy a car.

What Are Your Driving Needs?

Most families would probably answer this question in two different ways. They would look at how the car would be used for their social life (weekend activities and family obligations, for example), and how the car might be used for work (carpooling, driving clients around, etc.).

We needed an automobile that offered the same kind of carpooling flexibility that our van did—mainly, transporting seven people comfortably. In addition, my husband sometimes needed to pick up interview candidates at the airport or drive with colleagues to off-site meetings. So whichever car we chose not only needed the space for carpooling with kids and colleagues, but also needed to look halfway decent for work-related local travel.

What Are Your Safety Must-Haves?

Do you live in an area of the country where foul weather affects your ability to get around? When it snows or ices, the main road that runs through our hilly, two-stoplight town gets cleared. But every other road that leads up to it? That's a crapshoot. So, when it came time to look for a new car, four-wheel or all-wheel drive was a must.

What Kind of Fuel Efficiency Do You Desire?

Of course, we'd all love to be able to drive a hybrid vehicle that gets crazy-good miles to the gallon. But not everyone can afford a hybrid. In addition, most hybrids with eye-popping gas mileage are also small. Given the fact that I needed space for carpooling, a hybrid didn't make sense.

Of course, there are those SUV hybrids, which obviously seat more people. But when you look at their price tags and their gas mileage versus "regular" vehicles and their respective gas mileage, you could spend a lot less and get the same gas mileage with a car that isn't a hybrid.

Luckily for us, neither of us has a huge driving commute. Getting to my office means just going across the hall, and my husband's office is only twenty-five minutes away. For us, gas mileage isn't a really huge part of the equation. For others it might be, especially if your long commute involves travel on any roads that open "express" lanes for carpoolers or those driving a hybrid. But for us? Our only gas mileage requirement was that it be halfway decent—around the twenty-miles-per-gallon mark.

What's Your Budget?

I realize that the dollars and cents of getting a new car are really what counts in the long run. But you can't get to your final figure until you know ahead of time what your priorities are.

Beyond looking at our monthly expenses, we also did some homework on what cars with our "requirements" cost. We did this by looking at back issues of *Consumer Reports* at the library as well as by logging on to Edmunds.com, a website devoted to car buying and car ownership. This helped give us a sense of the financial neighborhood we needed to be in as far as monthly payments were concerned. Monthly payments would come into the picture should we decide to lease a car or get a car loan to pay for one. It also helped us get a good sense of a lump-sum amount we would need if we were going to buy the car outright.

Will You Lease, Buy New, or Buy Used?

Something else to add to your new-to-you car equation is buying new versus leasing new versus buying used. The folks at Edmunds.com recently crunched some numbers about the long-term cost of buying a new car versus leasing a new car versus buying a used car. (Still with me here?) And the dollars and cents that they came up with show how some of these car-ownership options just don't always make a lot of sense.

Remember: Being frugal isn't just about paying as little as possible. It's about getting the most bang for your buck. That's why Edmunds.com looked at the cost of first-year ownership (new or used) and the first year of a lease as well as the cost of owning a car after five years (new or used) and the cumulative cost of leasing a car after five years. These costs included:

- Down payment
- Car loan payments
- Insurance costs
- Maintenance and repairs
- Government charges through your Department of Motor Vehicles, Secretary of State, or whichever official office oversees car ownership and handles everything from licensing to license plates, sometimes called tags

Here are some numbers to consider, courtesy of Edmunds.com:

BUYING A NEW CAR VERSUS LEASING A NEW CAR VERSUS BUYING A USED CAR		
Option	**First-Year Ownership Costs**	**Five-Year Ownership Costs**
Buying a new car	$11,536	$32,388
Leasing a new car	$6,680	$32,140
Buying a used car	$6,570	$18,390

Clearly, buying a used car is the most frugal option if you're looking at your expenditures over a longer period of time. And it was raw numbers like these that led us to our decision to eventually buy a used, two-year-old Ford Freestyle (now known as the Taurus X) with 20,000 miles on it for about $20,000. The car came with leather seats, all-wheel drive, seating for seven, gas mileage ranging between 18 miles per gallon and 24 miles per gallon (not brilliant but good enough for us), and a DVD player.

As far as used cars being the better value, here's the one caveat that Edumunds.com throws into the equation: people who buy new cars are usually trading in cars that they originally bought new. This would mean that when it came time to trade in that bought-new car for a newer new car, the trade-in would have more value. Conversely, people who buy used cars would have a car that's worth less later on when they want to trade in that car for a newer car.

I can see the logic in this thinking if you're trading in for a new car every five or so years. But if you're a frugal car owner like I am, then you know that you've gotten all you can get out of your car when:

1. You've driven it into the ground so that it would need significant repairs to keep running.
2. The odometer has passed the 100,000-mile mark.
3. Both 1 and 2 above have happened!

Take us as an example. We knew we needed to trade in that minivan for a newer car: not only had it reached the 100,000-mile mark, but the transmission was in such dire straits that it was going to cost three times the van's value to fix it. Also, we'd bought that van new eight years earlier.

When we'd settled on buying the used Ford Freestyle, like many people, we decided to trade in our old car. But get this: the trade-in value for our bought-new van was only $1,000. In addition, the price we paid for our used car was thousands *less* than what we'd paid for that then-new van eight years earlier. Now that kind of math just doesn't add up if you're frugal like we are. Part of it has to do with depreciation—the value that your car *loses* over time.

In fact, if I had to do the whole buying a new-to-us car thing over again in the near future, I could easily see us going with the used-car option once more. I already know up-front that I'll get less when I trade in my used Ford Freestyle, but that doesn't worry me much, because I paid less for it in the first place.

Gas-Guzzler to Gas Sipper

While I wouldn't exactly call our Ford Freestyle a gas-guzzler, it's not exactly a gas sipper, either. But short of converting its engine to biodiesel, I can still make it the most fuel-efficient car that it can be. Anyone with a car that's not getting its optimal miles per gallon can try some of the following tricks to get as many miles as possible out of every drop of gas in their tank.

Practice Hypermiling Whenever Possible

By definition hypermiling means getting the most (hyper) mileage (miling) possible. Crazy folks who practice hypermiling do stupid things such as trying to draft behind large trucks and gliding on highways when they should be braking. No thanks—I'm not taking my life in my hands to eke out a better MPG, and neither should you.

There is one completely safe hypermiling trick I've used and would recommend with a clear conscience: pull through a parking spot so that you're facing outward to leave. If you park the traditional way, where you have to back out to drive away, you're using twice as much gas to get in and out of a parking spot. However, if you pull in nose first—and then pull all the way through—you can drive right out when you're done with your errands, thus saving you gas. Only drawback to this trick? Your trunk is never facing outward when you park at the supermarket and then need to load in groceries.

Be Efficient about How You Organize Your Errands

It's a fact that most cars get their worst gas mileage with around-town driving, what with all of the stopping and starting at traffic lights, or driving from parking lot to parking lot. The only cars that have improved gas mileage in these situations are hybrids. But errand running doesn't have to be a fuel-efficiency killer, even if you don't drive a hybrid.

If you piggyback your errands so that you can park once and then walk to the various stores you need to visit, obviously you'll use less fuel. (The fact that you'll sneak in some extra exercise doesn't hurt either.) Raise your hand if you've ever been guilty of, say, parking near the grocery store and then getting back into your car to drive to the dry cleaner on the other side of the shopping center. Not only is this lazy but it's a waste of gas. Trust me: you'll fill up your tank less often—and therefore spend less money—if you find ways to cut down on your stop-and-go driving.

Brake Less on the Highway

Naturally, if you find yourself in a potentially dangerous situation and you need to stop the car immediately, you should use the brake. However, you'll get better gas mileage overall if your car can maintain its speed over longer periods of time. Again, it's the accelerating and the stop-and-go stuff that make your car really guzzle the gas.

The first and best way to maintain your speed is to use cruise control (assuming your car has it). Here are two stats from Edmunds.com that illustrate this point.

1. If you are currently an aggressive driver (cruising at speeds from 75 to 85 mph, constantly accelerating and changing lanes and braking sharply) and you decided to calm down (driving with the cruise control set to 65 mph), your fuel economy would improve an average of 35 percent.
2. If you want to drive at higher speeds (77 mph with cruise control on) but you eliminate midrange acceleration, lane changes, and harsh braking, your fuel economy will improve an average of 12.5 percent.

SEAL OF APPROVAL *AUTOMATIC TOLL-PAYING DEVICE*

One way for you to cut down on stop-and-go driving when you're on a toll road is to spring for an automatic toll-paying device for your car. Where I live, it's called EZ Pass. In other states it might be called Fast Lane, I-Pass, or Sun Pass. They're all the same thing—a device you attach to the inside of your windshield or the front license plate of your car, and it sends a radio frequency to a tollbooth to "pay" your toll. (Our account, for example, is connected with a credit card so EZ Pass charges our card at the end of each month, based on the tollbooths we've passed through.)

Many of these lanes at tollbooths usually have shorter waits, if any at all. This has allowed us (and many other drivers with an EZ Pass or similar transponder) to avoid unnecessary idling and to enjoy discounts on toll fees. In addition, many highways have added express lanes that allow cars with EZ Pass and other toll-paying transponders to continue driving the speed limit as you pass under a "sign" on the road that does the toll reading for you.

Here's another benefit to using an automatic toll-paying device: you get a discount on the tolls themselves. These discounts vary based on the state where your program is based. Where I live, I can get $2 off any tolls paid during non-rush-hour times of the day. So thanks to the money, time, and gas that you save overall, that's why I'm giving a Suddenly Frugal Seal of Approval to automatic toll-paying devices.

Keep Your Tires Inflated

Tires that are low on air make your car drive less efficiently. Think about a basketball that needs a good pumping up. How does it perform on the court? Not well. Conversely, well-inflated tires can help up your gas mileage by as much as two miles per gallon.

Start with checking the air pressure in your tires. (You'll find their proper pounds per square inch, or psi, on the side of the tire itself, inside the driver's door jamb, or in the car's instruction manual.) If you don't have a tool that can check this at home, any service station should be able to help you. Tire pressure is important because, according to the Automobile Association of America, when your tires start losing air, you start losing fuel efficiency as well. That means you could blow through a tank of gas faster than you expect or want to, or can afford.

Well-Inflated Tires Could Save Your Life!

Besides increasing your fuel efficiency, properly inflated tires could save your life. According to the National Highway Traffic Safety Administration, underinflated tires (along with worn-out or simply old tires) are a leading cause of traffic accidents. That means that if you keep your tires properly inflated—and you replace them when they get worn out—you'll reduce your risk of a tire-caused traffic accident.

And having to pay for damage to your car, let alone any injuries you might sustain in a car accident, surely does not help when you're trying to live frugally. So in order to stay safe and save money, keep your tires inflated and in optimal condition.

Keep Your Engine Clean by Having the Filter Changed Regularly

In my old house, we discovered that even though the air filters in our forced-air heating/cooling system said they could be replaced every three months, we ended up having to change them every month. If we didn't, the air pretty much stopped flowing from the vents because the filter was gunked up with dust and dirt. Until we figured out the problem, we would crank up the heat in the winter just to get the house to a comfortable temperature, and in the summer we'd do the same cranking with the air conditioning system.

Instead of wasting money on heating and cooling, we should have just changed the filters sooner. Once we learned this trick, that's what we did. We could feel a marked difference in the air that came through the vents before and after a filter change.

Your car's engine air filter works the same way. When you don't replace the air filter, your car's performance can decrease by more than 10 percent, so says Fueleconomy.gov, a joint site of the U.S. Department of Energy's Office of Energy Efficiency and Renewable Energy and the U.S. Environmental Protection Agency. So, the next time you're in for an oil change, ask about having the air filter changed, too.

Secure Your Gas Cap

One of my special "talents" when it comes to car ownership is snapping gas-cap tethers. I've managed to do it with each of the cars we've owned. Then, without fail, I'll end up either driving away with the gas cap on the roof of the car (never to be seen again) or left behind at the gas station.

These days, I've learned always to check that the gas cap is back on as soon as I'm finished fueling. And it's a good thing I do, since I recently learned this interesting fact from Lauren Fix, known as the Car Coach: with a loose or missing gas cap, you lose gas to evaporation. Experts such as Fix say that in any given year, Americans might lose 147 million gallons of perfectly good gas, just because their gas cap was missing or not on tight enough.

To ensure that your gas doesn't turn to vapor and disappear, Fix recommends turning the cap at least three "clicks" to make sure it's securely closed. If your gas cap doesn't click, just be sure you've turned it enough times so that it feels tightly sealed. (You can get more car-care tips at Lauren Fix's website, *www.laurenfix.com*.)

Lighten Your Load as Much as Possible

When was the last time you took a look at what you've got stored in your trunk? Did you know that with extra weight in your car (not counting the passengers, I mean), the worse your gas mileage will be?

If you haven't bothered to clean out your trunk, then you are driving around extra loads that are literally weighing your car down. Got one of those minivans where you can take out the extra seats? When you don't need them, leave them behind in your garage so you can lighten your load and make your tank of gas last longer.

Carpool if You Can

Where I live, there are two kinds of carpooling. There is the traditional kind related to a job, and then there is the kind of carpooling that we moms get involved with. Here's why carpooling makes sense in a frugal world: the more we can share the driving, the less cash we'll spend on gas and on the maintenance of our collective cars. This means that our cars will last longer and we'll save money over time.

I realize that the concept of carpooling is not earth-shattering. But when was the last time you actually took advantage of a carpool opportunity to save money? If it's been awhile, give it a try. You just might like it, and so will your bottom line. Besides, when you're carpooling on a regular basis, it's a great incentive to keep your car clean and free of clutter that might be weighing it down and adversely affecting your gas mileage (as mentioned above).

Auto Maintenance

One of the best ways to ensure that you get the most out of any automobile that you own is to service it regularly. And no, you don't have to go to your dealer to get your regularly scheduled maintenance, unless something such as five years of free oil changes came with the purchase of your car. But otherwise any mechanic can give your car a checkup, and the guy at the corner gas station likely charges a lot less than the mechanics at the dealership.

If your car is still under warranty, though, it's a good idea to keep detailed records of your oil changes and other checkups and repairs. This will help if you have to submit a warranty claim at some point in the future. Speaking of warranties, if you do need a warranty repair or you receive a notice of a recall, then you should bring your car to the dealership for this kind of servicing. Otherwise, you'll be paying out of pocket for something that the dealership should cover for free.

Ways to Save on Auto Insurance

Even with all these tips for how to get more bang for your gas-mileage buck or how to find the most affordable car, there is still one more part to the frugal car ownership equation—car insurance. Luckily, you don't have to pay through the nose to insure your car if you consider the following four tips:

1. Maintain a clean driving record. Any accidents or speeding violations you get can increase your insurance premiums. Some companies even offer discounts on their rates if you're accident-free for a certain period of time.
2. Buy a car that insurance companies approve of. According to Allstate, a car's value, age, safety record, and repair history, as well as the likelihood that it could get stolen, can all affect your insurance premiums—to your benefit or as a liability. In addition, many states have determined that cars

with antilock brakes, air bags, and automatic seat belts are worthy of additional discounts.

As far as the whole "likelihood it could get stolen" part, depending on which website you read, there are a number of vehicles that crooks tend to like. Big SUVs seem to be a popular target, as are big trucks (think Ford 350) as well as some of the most popular sedans on the road, such as the Toyota Camry and the Honda Civic. Go figure.

3. Bundle and automate your insurance premiums. Two of the best ways to get discounts on your car insurance rates are to sign up for automatic payment through your bank and to get all of your insurance needs—home, life, and auto—through a single provider. Insurance rates can often be discounted by as much as 10 percent when you bundle the various policies under one umbrella.
4. Rethink your coverage as your car ages. When you insure a brand-new car, you want to make sure that your policy is good enough to cover the value of the car should you have an accident. However, as your car ages, it loses its value. So if you own an older car, it's a good idea to rethink things such as your collision coverage (which covers damage to your car from an accident) as well as comprehensive coverage (the part of an insurance policy that pays to fix a broken windshield, for example, not associated with a crash).

Consumer Reports recommends that you keep a ten-to-one ratio in mind when thinking about changing your insurance. That is, if your car is worth $10,000, you should be paying about one-tenth of that—or $1,000 a year—for the collision and comprehensive portions of your auto insurance.

This is something we considered in the last year that we owned the minivan. When the minivan's value dropped to

$1,500 but our insurance premiums were still above that ten-to-one ratio (or more than $150), we decided it made financial sense for us to drop collision and comprehensive coverage on that car.

Keep in mind that you should discuss all of your state's auto insurance requirements with your insurance agent, and then make the decision based on his or her recommendation, your car's value, and your budget.

Total Savings in This Chapter

Probably the biggest piece of take-away money-saving advice from this chapter is this: When it comes time to buy a new car, don't immediately think about buying new or leasing new. As I mentioned in the previous pages, when you look at the cost of ownership in the first five years that you have a car, you quickly see how much more expensive buying or leasing a new car can be.

Possible savings in Chapter 6:
$14,000 a year
during the first five years of owning a used car

chapter seven

THE WARM AND COLD OF IT

One of the biggest money-suckers in a household budget is heating and cooling. This is usually because people don't know how to run their heating or air conditioning systems at an optimal efficiency level, or their house is energy-inefficient to begin with. No sweat. In this chapter, I'll help you understand how you can open up or close off your home so you can achieve maximum heating and cooling. In addition, I'll discuss the different ways that people heat their homes—and how you can make whatever energy source you use work the best for you. Plus, I'll explain how windows and doors can affect your energy bills, and not always in a positive way.

Air Conditioning

If you've ever doubted the value of shade in reducing your need for air conditioning, try this one hot day: park your car in a shady spot while you go shopping or do another errand that will keep you out of your car for a few hours. When you get back to your car and it's still in the shade, it will be significantly cooler inside the car than it is outside. You don't have to have an advanced degree in science to figure out why your car stayed cool: the trees shaded it from direct sunlight. Well, guess what? The same principle applies to your home on hot days.

If you've got shade trees planted on your property, you know what I'm talking about. They usually allow your home to remain cool even when it's boiling hot outside. If you don't have shade trees and you're looking to redo your landscaping, think about planting some deciduous trees (they're the ones that lose their leaves in winter) on the southern and eastern sides of your home, the sides that get the most sunlight. (See Chapter 10, "In the Garden and Around the Yard," for more on this topic.)

If you don't have any of these kinds of trees to work with, you can create shade by closing shades, curtains, and blinds during the hottest parts of the day. This way your home won't bake when it's hot outside, and you won't have to crank the a/c to cool down a room that's burning up from sunlight.

Window Air Conditioners Versus Central Systems

How do you determine if you should use a window air conditioning unit versus central air in your home? You should consider several things:

1. The climate where you live
2. How your home is insulated
3. The size of your home
4. Your budget
5. Your personal preferences

Let's look at each.

CLIMATE

If you're looking to cool your home and lower the humidity, a central air conditioning system is your best bet, hands down, as far as efficiency goes. There are two reasons that window units are all wet when it comes to reducing humidity: First, they tend to sweat (especially if they are overworked) and therefore introduce moisture into the room. And, second, since it's harder to seal window units, they tend to let hot, humid air in from the outside, which pretty much negates the dehumidifying effect of the air conditioner.

That said, if humidity isn't your problem and you'd just like to cool your home, you could get away with one window unit on each floor. This is assuming that your home is well insulated and small enough for one window unit to do the job.

INSULATION

As far as insulation is concerned, I'm not just talking about the stuff that's in your walls. I'm talking about well-insulated windows, doors, and, believe it or not, your attic—assuming you live in a house or apartment that has one. The attic becomes a key component in cooling your home for this reason alone: during the summer, the temperature in an attic can climb to well over 100 degrees. And even though you were brought up to believe that hot air rises, unfortunately, hot attics can affect how cool the upper floors of a house remain. So though your air conditioner is humming along and keeping the first floor of your house comfortable, this constant flow of heat from the attic can bake your bedrooms upstairs.

Although most people don't think of insulation as a way to keep cool, increasing levels in your attic can make a huge difference. The rule of thumb for insulation is this: when you go up into your attic, if you can see the floor joists (the beams of wood) sticking up over the insulation in the floor, you need more insulation.

THE SIZE OF YOUR HOUSE

The other key component in buying a window air conditioner is making sure you match the square footage of the space you're looking to cool. Check out the Energy Star website at *www.energystar.gov* to figure out the right-sized air conditioner based on a room's size.

YOUR BUDGET

Window units are going to be cheaper than installing central air. However, if you're going to purchase more than a few of these units so you can cool down a number of rooms in your home—and you have the option of installing central air conditioning—you're probably better off going with a central air system. That's because a central air unit will use less energy overall and cool more efficiently than a series of window units running in tandem.

PERSONAL PREFERENCES

Finally, air conditioning and keeping cool can be all about personal preferences. When my husband and I first had kids and we weren't making a lot of money, it wasn't such a huge sacrifice to use only one window air conditioning unit—in the master bedroom. On brutally hot nights, we'd all just bunk in our bedroom, and we survived just fine like that for a number of years. It was only when we moved to a new and bigger house—and the kids got older and bigger, too—that we realized we'd achieve better long-term comfort and happiness if we stepped up to a central air system.

Tips for Keeping Cool

Air conditioning talk aside, following are three tips for keeping your home cool.

1. Limit the number of lights you have on during hot days. Unless you've replaced all of your incandescent bulbs with compact fluorescent lights (see page 117), your lights are going to be giving off heat the longer they stay on. If you're trying to keep cool inside, keep the lights off for as long as possible.
2. Don't cook inside on hot days. While meal planning and cooking at home is a huge part of living frugally, during the summer you may need to switch things up a bit so you can keep your stove and oven off during the hottest days. When it is boiling outside, you don't want to boil water on your stovetop. Instead, try to use appliances that don't give off a lot of heat, such as the microwave or a slow cooker, or use your grill outside.
3. Keep window treatments closed during the heat of the day. This tip is pretty simple and straightforward—if the sun can't get into your house because the windows are blocked off, then you won't have to deal with passive heating.

Heating Systems

On sunny winter days, know what I do? Throw open the curtains, pull up the shades, and move all of the window treatments to the side so that the bright sunshine can come streaming into my home. If you're looking for an easy way to warm your house without raising your heating bills, consider taking advantage of Mother Nature's heating system—the sun. Of course, the trick is keeping your window treatments open during the sunniest parts of the days, and then closing them up when the sun fades so that you don't lose any of that warmth.

But unless you have a solar heating system for your home, Mother Nature can't do all of the heating for you. Obviously, you're going to have to rely on your good old furnace, oil boiler, or other heating system for keeping your home warm. And with prices trending upward for the three most popular kinds of heat energy sources—oil, gas, and electricity—you may be wondering what you could possibly do to keep your heating bills in check. Well, I've got good news. You can control (a bit) how much you spend heating your home, regardless of which energy source you use, in a number of ways.

Making Your Home More Energy Efficient

Here's the bottom line on keeping your home warm: prevent heat loss throughout your house. If you can do this, then you will likely see your energy costs going down. Here's how to prevent heat loss:

- Reinsulate your attic.
- Use weather stripping to plug up any drafts you find around door edges.
- Place draft "dodgers" (also known as draft stoppers) or even rolled-up throw rugs, towels, or blankets on the floor in front of drafty doors.
- Install storm windows over existing windows. These provide an additional barrier against air escaping from your house or the cold/warm air outside getting in.

- Caulk around any cracks or holes you find in the various windows around the house.
- Keep window treatments closed to prevent heat from leaking out of poorly insulated windows.

In addition to the proactive fixes to prevent heat loss, you can take some personal steps to use less heat in the winter. These include:

- Putting down rugs so that smooth floors don't feel as cold to the touch
- Wearing socks
- Adding an extra layer to your body—whether it be a sweater or a fleece blanket
- Moving furniture you sit or sleep on away from exterior walls so you're farther away from the cold

Making Your Heating System Run More Efficiently

According to Ken Ely, a heating products manager for Lennox Industries, a company that manufactures heating and cooling systems, people need to think of their heating system as they do their car. "We all like to take our automobile in for regular tuneups so that it runs optimally and uses as little gas as possible," he says. "Well, your furnace is the same. If you do an annual clean and tuneup, your furnace will be running at top efficiency and will use as little energy as possible."

In fact, it seems that an annual furnace cleaning is the one thing most homeowners just push to the back burner, saying, "Oh, I'll get to that later." But like pushing off seeing the dentist, only to discover multiple cavities when you finally do go, forgoing your furnace's annual cleaning can lead to big problems down the road. And I mean big, *costly* problems.

For example, when we moved into our house and had our oil boiler cleaned and serviced—and the attached chimney cleaned and inspected—we discovered a dirty little secret: the previous owners had neglected this kind of servicing for years. Because of that, the chimney was caked with soot and starting to disintegrate. Had the house gone another year without a cleaning, the chimney could have caught on fire and/or the entire inside of the chimney would have crumbled—literally fallen to pieces. The cost to replace something like a boiler chimney? Easily $3,000!

Regardless of what energy source you use to run your furnace, you should pay to have it cleaned and serviced every year to avoid big headaches down the road. Additionally, keeping it clean will keep it running more efficiently.

Here are other ways to keep your heating system running efficiently—and as inexpensively as possible.

CHANGE FILTERS REGULARLY

Most forced-air heating systems have a slot for a removable filter that you should change regularly. If you don't, you will reduce the airflow output from the system and make your system work harder to keep your home warm. This, in turn, will use more energy in the long run than if you just changed the darned filter on a regular basis. What does "regular basis" mean for you? That depends on your home. In my old house, which had a forced-air system, we used filters that said they could last for up to three months. However, we ended up needing to change them monthly because our house was dusty and because we have a dog. (His hair alone created debris that could potentially get trapped in the forced-air system.) According to the experts at Lowe's, replacing your air filter regularly can save you $100 a year in heating and cooling bills.

KEEP HEATING ELEMENTS IN THE HOUSE CLEAR AND CLEAN

If you have a forced-air system, it's a good idea to vacuum out the register covers on the vents whenever you're vacuuming your house. As with the filter, anything that gets trapped in the covers will lessen the amount of heated air that gets into a room. Similarly, if you have a baseboard heating system, make sure that you keep them clean of dust, dirt, and cobwebs. Because heated water moves through the baseboards and that's how it gives off heat, if the baseboards themselves are caked in grime, you won't be getting as much heat as you possibly can from them. And as with any other inefficient, dirty heating system, you'll end up turning up the heat—and paying more in the end to heat your home—just to get it to a comfortable temperature.

Shop for a New System in the Off-Season

If you need to buy a new furnace, the experts at Trane (maker of heating and cooling systems) suggest you shop in the off-season. You have a better chance of getting a deal on air conditioners during the winter and furnaces in the summer.

Your Thermostat and You

A piece of frugal advice that's a no-brainer is to get a programmable thermostat for both your heating and cooling. The idea behind a programmable thermostat is that you set it to change the temperature in your house based on whether or not you are home and/or asleep. For example, during the winter, we have our programmable thermostat set to go down to sixty-four degrees around eleven o'clock at night—a time by which everyone is in bed. Around six-thirty in the morning, the thermostat is programmed to kick back on and go up to sixty-nine degrees. This warms the house up for when we're all getting up, dressed, and ready for the day. Because I work at home, I keep the temperature comfortable while I'm here. Though experts say that you can achieve energy- and cost-savings by adjusting your thermostat for as little as four hours a day, I will manually turn the heat back down to the overnight level to save energy even if I'm leaving the house for only an hour or two. Every little bit helps, right?

In homes where everyone leaves for school or their job, it makes sense to program the thermostat to go back down to a lower temperature while everyone is away. Then, about thirty minutes before people start coming home, the thermostat can kick in once again to a warmer temperature so that the house is comfortable by the time everyone arrives home. (Of course, in the summer, the reverse happens with the air conditioning. You program the thermostat to be warmer during the overnight and away hours, and cooler when people are home.)

Some people believe that raising and lowering the thermostat throughout the day means you're using more energy. They think that their cooling or heating system will have to work harder to get the temperature back to a comfortable place when they return—therefore using extra energy in the process. This means that whatever energy they may have saved by turning off the air conditioner or changing the thermostat setting, they've now used up in cooling off or heating up the home.

That is, in fact, not true. Every reliable source (e.g., government or respectable energy website) I could find says that the exact opposite happens. They show that if you fiddled around with your thermostat as I've described above, you would actually save money in the long run. According to Energy Star this trick can help you save as much as 10 percent on your annual energy bills.

SEAL OF APPROVAL *CEILING FANS*

If you're a fan of home makeover shows on HGTV and TLC, you know that one of the first things designers ditch in a home they're redoing is the ceiling fan. But although ceiling fans may not be the most aesthetically pleasing item in a room, they can contribute greatly to reduced energy bills. That's because a ceiling fan turned on in the summer can cool the inside of your home without your having to adjust the temperature on the air conditioner. How? Because the fan circulates the air in the room. Just the act of air moving over your skin cools you down, because it increases evaporation. This make you feel cooler, even though you haven't touched the air conditioner.

Some experts estimate that using a ceiling fan can help you save up to $500 a year on heating and cooling costs. Plus, ceiling fans use very little energy, and they don't cost too much to buy and install. That's why I'm giving a Suddenly Frugal Seal of Approval to ceiling fans.

Moving Hot or Cold Air Around

You can find Energy Star–rated ceiling fans, if you're in the market for a new one. Just remember that ceiling fans cool the body, not the temperature in the room, so make sure you turn them off when you leave a room. Leaving them on will only waste energy (albeit small amounts of energy) and won't make the room any cooler for when you return.

Here are a few other notes about fans:

- If it's been awhile since you last turned on a ceiling fan, give it a good dusting before you power it up. If you skip the dusting part, you're going to send dust particles flying around your room. Plus, like other gunked-up appliances, your ceiling fan may not operate at its fullest capacity if dust and debris weigh down the blades.
- Other kinds of fans can help to cool or heat a room. If you don't have a ceiling fan installed, you can try a box or desktop fan—especially if you can get the oscillating kind (the one that turns from side to side).
- You can run the fan-only option in your central air system when you have the heat on in the winter to warm your house. This is useful if you are using a solitary source of heat—say a pellet stove or a wood stove in one room—that is not connected to the "regular" heating system you use (baseboard heating, for example). The air movement will help spread the heat to other rooms in the house.

Lighting the Right Way

I never realized how much our lighting affected how much we paid for energy until we made a change to how we used lighting and what kind of lighting we used. In our old house, we paid hundreds and hundreds of dollars in electrical costs each month. I guess, looking back, that really shouldn't surprise me since our house was always lit up like a Christmas tree. When we moved into our new house and decided to adopt our frugal ways, one of the first things we changed was our relationship with lights. For starters, we got everyone in the habit of turning off lights when they left a room. It took a couple of weeks before turning lights off became second nature. Then we tackled the type of light bulbs we used.

Use CFLs

We removed all of our incandescent light bulbs—the traditional Thomas Edison–designed light bulbs—and replaced them with compact fluorescent lights (CFLs), which are the twisty light bulbs you see in stores these days. (Some are made to look like the more traditional bulbs now, too.) While our up-front cost for the compact fluorescent lights was a bit higher than expected, it was money well spent.

I'd read that these newer fluorescent bulbs last ten times longer than traditional light bulbs—the U.S. Department of Energy's Office of Energy Efficiency and Renewable Energy (the EERE) says that each bulb lasts about 10,000 hours. Well, you know what? I believe it. It's been more than two years since we moved into this house, and I've yet to replace a burned-out compact fluorescent light bulb.

In addition to lasting longer, these light bulbs give off less heat—again, the EERE says the bulbs produce 90 percent less heat than traditional bulbs—which means that when we do have the lights on during warm days, the bulbs aren't contributing to the heat in the room. And here's the best part: compact fluorescent bulbs may give off the same amount of light as traditional light bulbs (albeit the color can look a bit different and does take some getting used to), but they use one-quarter of the energy of other bulbs.

As far as outdoor lighting goes, you should try to swap traditional bulbs for the fluorescent kind to save money in the long run as well. (Be sure you buy CFLs meant for outdoor use.) However, if that's not feasible, at the very least invest in motion-detector sensors for outside. This way, if you leave the outdoor lights on with more expensive bulbs in them, they'll only turn on when something moves outside—such as your car pulling into the driveway. That will definitely save you money in the long run.

Don't Throw CFLs in the Trash

While compact fluorescent bulbs make perfect sense in a frugal household, you've got to think green when it comes to disposing of them. CFLs contain trace amounts of mercury, which is damaging to the earth should they end up in landfills. That's why you can't just throw them in the garbage. Instead, you must dispose of your CFLs with a certified recycler. Two national retailers have stepped up to recycle CFLs for free: IKEA and Home Depot. If by some chance you do not live near either of these stores, you can log on to Earth 911 (*www.earth911.org*) to find a recycler near you. Also good to know: when your state, county, or town holds one of those household hazardous waste recycling days, you can bring CFLs with you.

Here's another way we try to use lights less often so we can pay less for our energy: we play a game with ourselves of seeing how long we can go during the day without turning on the lights. Instead, we rely on natural light from outside to illuminate the inside. There are days that I can put on my makeup without the lights on, load and unload the dishwasher, and read the morning paper with nary a light on.

If you must turn on the lights, then turn on the smallest one possible. In my kitchen, for example, the counters themselves are kind of dark. So we installed inexpensive fluorescent, under-cabinet lighting. This way I can switch on just a single light to illuminate a counter rather than turning on the big overhead light.

I take a similar approach in my home office. Instead of having a big light on, I use two smaller desk lamps, and keep the shades on the window open. Together this provides plenty of light for me to work during the day without running up my electric bills.

Total Savings in This Chapter

As with your car, regular maintenance is critical to keep your home's heating and cooling systems running efficiently. Though you may save money in the short run by putting off paying for a furnace cleaning, for example, that decision will come back to haunt you financially in the long run. Remember my oil boiler situation and the almost-crumbling chimney? By spending a few hundred dollars each year to have my boiler and chimney cleaned, I've saved myself from having to spend $3,000 for a new system and replacement chimney. Other savings you can realize by following the advice in this chapter include nearly $700 in energy savings from using a programmable thermostat as well as a ceiling fan to keep you cool without touching the air conditioner.

Possible savings in Chapter 7: close to $4,000 a year

chapter eight

BECOMING A DO-IT-YOURSELFER

One of the best ways to embrace frugality is to learn how to become a self-sufficient person. I'm not talking about getting "off the grid" but rather learning how to do things for yourself, from easy home repairs to mending clothing to making your own cleaners. This chapter offers advice on how you can learn new skills at a low cost or for free along with some of the common DIY things you can do around the house to save yourself big bucks. Remember that old adage "Give a man a fish and you feed him for a day. Teach a man to fish and you feed him for a lifetime"? Well, the same applies to learning new DIY skills. Once you have the know-how under your belt for how to fix, mend, or clean things, you'll never have to pay someone to do it for you again.

Make Your Own Home Cleaners

Do you have any idea how much you must spend each year on products to clean your house? All I know is that since I've started making my own home cleaners, I haven't had to buy glass cleaner or products to mop the floor in months, maybe even years.

Believe it or not, there are items that you probably already own that can do double duty as cleaners for your home. Just walk into your kitchen, open your pantry, and take a look around. You probably have two things right there that can clean plenty of areas of your home: vinegar and baking soda. Here are some ways you can add vinegar and baking soda to your cleaning repertoire.

Vinegar Is a Great Floor and Window Cleaner

If you have hardwood floors like I do, you'll love how well a mixture of vinegar and water can clean your floors. I swear this combination is better than any store-bought cleaner I've ever found. And it's cheap, too. A 128 fluid-ounce bottle of store-brand distilled white vinegar (the kind I recommend you use for cleaning) cost me about $1.50. If I were to purchase a similar size bottle of a commercial cleaner at a warehouse store, I would pay twenty to thirty times more. Just be sure you dilute the vinegar with enough water (one part vinegar to about ten parts of water, or something similar), so you can avoid damaging your floors and making your house smell like a salad bar.

Vinegar Can "Fix" a Pet's Accidents

Thankfully, my dog has never been skunked, but lots of people have told me that if Fido gets a little too friendly with Pepe Le Pew, vinegar can help to get skunk odor out of his fur.

If your dog or cat has an accident on the rug, vinegar can help you out as well. Vinegar removes the odor from the carpet and, experts tell me, the vinegar smell itself is so repulsive to the animals that they won't pee there again. So it's a deodorizer and a repellant all wrapped up in one!

Vinegar Can Help Clean Out Appliances

My mother taught me to use vinegar as a way to clean out the gunk in my coffee machine without poisoning myself in the process. Just fill the water receptacle with vinegar and "brew" until the pot is filled. Then run three or four more pots of water through the coffee machine to make sure all the vinegar is gone from the system. I'll bet it will be worth your time, and you'll see how your coffee brewing time speeds up after this kind of cleaning.

Vinegar Deodorizes Smelly Laundry

If you've ever left a load of laundry in a closed washing machine for too long, then you know how musty it can smell after sitting around wet. To get rid of that musty smell, add 1 cup of vinegar to the washing machine in lieu of laundry detergent, and run the laundry through once more on a short cycle. This should take the laundry from smelling yucky to not smelling like anything at all.

In addition to fixing entire loads of smelly laundry, vinegar works on individual items—such as my daughter's soccer cleats. At the end of the last soccer season, I thought those cleats would be smelly forever—they smelled like the inside of a litter box. Even the dog, who loves to steal shoes to play with them, was staying away from these cleats. When no amount of airing them out or washing and rewashing was helping, I gave vinegar a try. I washed the cleats with a generous amount of vinegar—at least a cup of vinegar added to the washing machine as it filled. After letting the cleats dry on the line, they were much improved. While they didn't smell like a bunch of flowers, at least they didn't trigger my gag reflex anymore.

Vinegar and Baking Soda Are Great for Clearing Clogs

I mean drain clogs in pipes, of course, not clog-style shoes. You put about ½ cup of baking soda into the clogged drain, then pour enough vinegar to cover the baking soda. As it bubbles up, it will help to clear the drain.

Stone and Vinegar Don't Mix

While vinegar makes a great, all-purpose cleaner in your home, there are certain items in your home that you should *not* use vinegar on. This would include anything that is made of stone, whether it be travertine floors or marble countertops, or other natural, porous materials such as ceramic tile or granite. Because vinegar is an acid, it could damage any surface made with these materials. So though vinegar is a frugal cleaner, if you use it on these surfaces and damage them, you may end up having to spend more to replace the damaged tile or stone.

This is another trick that I can thank my dear old mother for. Sometimes you have to add in a few extra steps, in the form of a plunger to loosen the clog in the pipes, and maybe pour a teakettle's worth of boiling water down the drain. But in the end, I guarantee that the clog will clear. Not only will you have saved money by not buying a commercial clog clearer, but you will have spared your pipe, septic tank, or sewer system from those toxic chemicals.

Baking Soda as a Scouring Agent

If you have hard water like I do, you know how icky the side of your tub can get from those white hard-water stains. Instead of turning to store-bought scouring agents to get that grime out of the tub or shower, try baking soda and elbow grease, with a sponge with a scrubbing side to it. You'll have a sparkling tub in no time.

DIY Laundry Detergent

As with many things having to do with frugality, you often have to invest some time to get a greater return on your investment in saving money. While making my own laundry detergent wasn't super-time-consuming, it definitely involved more effort than just unscrewing the cap on a detergent bottle. But I'm glad I learned how to make DIY laundry soap, and here's how you can make it, too.

I created this recipe after reading lots of different variations of DIY laundry detergent on the web. I decided to focus on a dry detergent recipe, which seemed much easier than the liquid detergent recipes I found. Before I got started I located a 32-ounce storage container.

1. **Start with two parts washing soda.**
   I scooped out 2 cups of washing soda. Note: washing soda is not the same as baking soda. Don't make the mistake I did and assume you would find washing soda alongside baking soda in the baking aisle. You have to look in the laundry aisle of a grocery store to find it.

2. **Add two parts Borax.**
   I took the literal approach with 2 cups like I did with the washing soda. You can find Borax in the laundry aisle as well.
3. **Add one part grated or chopped Fels-Naptha soap.**
   I'd read that some people put the soap in a food processor to get it into tiny bits; instead I used a cheese grater/press that is designed to shred Parmesan cheese—you may have seen a waiter using one of these in an Italian restaurant. I just replaced the hunk of Parmesan with Fels-Naptha soap. Fels-Naptha soap should be located near the Borax and washing soda in the laundry aisle. If you can't find it, Ivory soap or even those little bars of soap that you pick up as a hotel guest would work as well.
4. **Mix all ingredients.**
   Nothing fancy here. I put the top on the storage container and gave it a few shakes. You could stir it with a spoon, too.

It took me five minutes to put this all together. Really, only five minutes. Grating the soap is what took the longest. When it was time to do the laundry, I measured out ¼ cup of the detergent. (I keep that measuring cup in the container with the detergent for easier laundry-doing in the future.) Because this homemade detergent may need more time to dissolve in a top-loading washing machine, I recommend pouring it in first and then letting the water fill about one-quarter of the way before adding clothes. The only difference I found from commercial laundry detergents? No bubbles. But the cleaning ability was the same.

Other people who have tried my recipe (which I originally posted on my blog) have told me that this DIY laundry soap works in both hot and cold washes, as well as in both top- and front-loading washing machines.

Bottom line: DIY laundry detergent supplies cost me about $6 up-front. One batch lasted a few weeks, and when it ran out, I whipped up some more.

STAIN REMOVAL TECHNIQUES

Now that I'm making my own laundry detergent, here's what I miss about not having a liquid detergent to use—my inability to pour it on my husband's "ring around the collar" stains on his work shirts. (I'm still scarred by those "ring around the collar" Wisk commercials from the 1970s.) But here's what I've discovered: if I wet the collar and then rub the Fels-Naptha soap on the stains—kind of like a bar version of a Spray 'n Wash stick—it helps to get the stains out.

I've also learned that pretreating a stain with shampoo works equally well—especially with ring-around-the-collar stains. Just buy the cheapest clarifying shampoo you can find to use on stains. Why clarifying? Because it is designed to remove built-up residue on your hair and give it a "deep clean," and it seems to work the same way on built-in stains on clothes.

Do Your Own Dry Cleaning

Before going suddenly frugal, we were spending about $30 a month having my husband's shirts and suits sent to the cleaner. Yeah, $30 a month is no big deal—that's $1 a day. But if you look at it from an annual cost, that's $360 that we might have saved if we didn't use the dry cleaner. It was a no-brainer to cut out the dry cleaner. Yes, it was convenient to shove our dry cleaning into a laundry bag, and put it out on the step (the dry cleaner offered door-to-door service) twice a week. My husband's shirts came home clean and pressed, and his suits were always crisp and ready to be worn. But this was a time saver, not a money saver. And while my time is important, at this point in my life saving my money is more important.

Washing and Ironing Dress Shirts

I started washing my husband's shirts with the rest of the laundry. When they were washed, I would put the shirts in the dryer for five minutes to get out the wrinkles, and then I would hang them up. Lucky for me, most of his shirts are the wash-and-wear, wrinkle-resistant kind. That meant that by the time they dried on the hanger, they looked good enough to wear. Sure, there wasn't that telltale crease along the arms that say "just ironed," but so what. For his shirts that were not wrinkle resistant, I would spend about thirty to forty minutes one weekend day ironing them. I usually did this while catching up on some TV.

SEAL OF APPROVAL *DRYEL KIT*

Just because we gave up on using the dry cleaner doesn't mean that we've given up on keeping our dry clean–only garments clean. These days we're cleaning them at home as well, thanks to our Dryel kit. It comes with a plastic garment bag that does a sort of mock dry cleaning of your clothes by using the heat of the dryer, so says the Dryel website (*www.dryel.com*). (Go there for a $3 off coupon, by the way.)

Here's how I use it to clean my husband's suits. I put his suit jacket and pants (no more than four pieces at a time) in the Dryel bag that comes with a starter kit, and then I put a Dryel "wet wipe" in with the clothes. I zip the bag closed and put it in the dryer, on medium heat, for thirty minutes. His suits come out damp and "freshened." Then I hang them up to dry.

I've found Dryel to be a great stopgap measure for increasing the time between sending a suit to the dry cleaner, thus saving me money in the long run. That's why I'm giving Dryel a Suddenly Frugal Seal of Approval.

Benefits of At-Home Dry Cleaning

In a perfect world you should be dry cleaning a suit no more than twice a year anyway. Some style experts suggest using a soft brush to sweep away any debris on a suit rather than sending it off to the dry cleaner. Plus, frequent dry cleaning can make fabric brittle and weak. This might explain why the cotton on some of my husband's dry-cleaned work shirts seems to be eroding—almost as if moths have been eating it. (We don't have a moth problem.)

I believe that by cutting out the dry cleaner, I've achieved two money-saving goals:

1. I've saved about $360 a year in dry cleaning costs.
2. I've extended the life of my husband's work clothes, which means I'll have to replace them less often. Before, he would need new work shirts each year. Because my husband is considered "big and tall," we always paid more for his work clothes. However, since we gave up the dry cleaner and starting to launder his clothes at home, his shirts have been lasting longer. That saves me money since he keeps ten shirts in rotation (enough for two weeks of workdays) and his shirts cost, on average, about $50. Merely by changing how we launder his shirts, we are saving as much as $500 every year.

All told, our decision to give up the dry cleaner has, potentially, saved us $860 a year. That's nothing to sneeze at.

Learning Skills the Old-School Way

When you were a little kid and you wanted to learn how to do something, you went to a class or lessons to learn that skill. Adults can do the same, but sometimes we forget! Now's the time to renew your interest in classes and new skills so you, too, can become a DIYer. The idea here is simple: If you know how to do things such as paint a wall or sew a hem, then you don't have to hire a painter or a tailor. You could do both yourself, which is obviously a huge cost savings.

The trick is figuring out which skills you're lacking and which you're willing to learn. Start by reviewing your credit card statements or checking account and seeing if you can uncover certain areas of your life where you've been "outsourcing" household tasks. You may discover that, in addition to dry cleaning, you may have been using outside sources to mend your clothing, repair things around your house, or groom your pet. Here are some ideas on where you can go to learn those new skills to save you money in the long run.

Skill-Sharing Groups

You may find "skill swapping" workshops in your area, which is kind of like bartering your talent to teach others what you know and they, in turn, will teach *you* what *they* know. There are "skill-share" groups popping up all over the country; there may be one of these free events near you. If not, you could try organizing an informal group with family and friends.

Home Improvement

Every time I walk into a Home Depot or Lowe's, I notice the signs that promote the upcoming DIY workshops that the store is offering. These are free, in-store classes that are designed to turn any homebody into a DIY pro. Turns out you can log on to find out about these courses and skills, too.

On *www.homeimproverclub.com*, for example, you can search, via zip code, for Home Depot classes in three categories: weekly workshops, Do-It-Herself workshops, and kids' workshops. Here's something even cooler—some of these clinics are now offered online as video tutorials. Think of it as do-it-yourself for the YouTube crowd.

Lowe's offers a similar online option—a library on its *www.lowes.com* website of "how-to projects."

Another resource for DIY classes on home improvement is the local cooperative extension office of your state university. Through these offices, you can learn about nearly anything having to do with the outdoors (that is, gardening and landscaping).

Sewing and Mending

Unless you plan to attend home economics classes again (they're now called "family and consumer science" in our school district), you're not going to be able to find any "learn to sew" classes for free. But I'll bet you can find one of these classes for not a lot of money at your local community college or even house of worship.

If none of those resources come through for you, you can always turn to your local crafts store. Jo-Ann Fabric and Craft stores run classes from time to time on various topics. For example, through its Jo-Ann Creative University, you could sign up for three different levels of sewing classes or upholstery classes.

The latter is a terrific option if you need to fix up a piece of furniture or a window treatment and don't want to pay someone to do it for you. And these classes are affordable. Sewing 101, for example, costs only $35. You'd pay at least that getting two or so pairs of pants hemmed at the tailor; you'll make back your investment in this class in no time. (Unfortunately, as of this writing, Michaels craft stores have suspended all DIY classes except for cake decorating. So unless you need to learn how to decorate wedding or special-occasion cakes on the cheap, Michaels won't be able to help you learn any new DIY skills.)

Making Jewelry

A few years ago my husband taught my daughter how to make earrings. Yes, you read that right, my husband—not I—taught her. You see, he'd made earrings in college and sold them to his dorm-mates as a way of making extra cash. (It helped that he went to a predominantly female college.) When my daughter was looking for ways to earn money and satisfy her love of jewelry without going broke, he showed her how easy it was to put together a pair of earrings. We've been drowning in crystal beads, wire hoops, and pliers (which double as wire-cutters) ever since. And when she gets a craving for new jewelry, instead of spending money at the store, she makes something for herself.

Here's another benefit to her jewelry-making skills: whenever my daughter needs to buy a gift, she makes one instead. For a few years running, her gift of choice for the female educators in her life has been a pair of earrings. Also, she likes to give her friends earrings or a handmade bracelet when she's invited to a birthday party. Given my daughter's limited income (her monthly allowance), her knowing how to make jewelry has allowed her to create inexpensive yet memorable gifts for lots of different people, myself included. Think about how you, too, might benefit from knowing how to make your own jewelry.

Cooking

Let's say that you want to learn to cook more efficiently, how to use your slow cooker, or discover a kitchen skill you don't have. If you checked out local adult education classes or even the continuing education classes at your community college, you might find the classes you're looking for. Even a local cookware store or restaurant may offer free or affordable classes that will make you a master chef—or at least a reasonable facsimile.

A friend of mine took a class on canning and preserving at a local community college many years ago, and she's still using the skills she learned there. During the fall she is busy with her fruit and vegetable harvest, putting together a winter-long supply of home-canned jams, jellies, pickles, relishes, tomato sauce, tomatoes, and applesauce. Not only does this save her from having to buy these products at the store, but whenever she needs to bring a hostess gift or find a last-minute birthday gift, she's got something yummy and homemade on hand.

Computer Skills

Though I didn't embrace my inner frugality until a few years ago, I can point to thrifty tendencies among my past habits. Take designing a website. Ten years ago, when I realized that I needed to have a website to promote my writing business, I wasn't about to hire someone to build me a site. I was going to do it myself. Which is why I signed up for a basic HTML class at my community college. For about $75 and four nights of my time, I acquired basic HTML knowledge. In addition, thanks to membership in a professional organization, I qualified for super-cheap web hosting because I was able to build my website myself. If you've been paying someone to be your tech guy—whether to build a website or repair problems—why not invest a little money in learning this skill yourself?

Additionally, if you happen to own an Apple computer, you can sign up for free classes through the Apple store to learn how to use your computer to work with photos, video, music, website, and design. These latter skills are great to know if you happen to run your own business and want to keep your outsourcing costs to a minimum.

Holiday Cards and Greetings

Are you one of those families that just has to have a family portrait with your holiday cards each year? If you are and you hire someone to shoot your family picture, then you know that, even with a good deal, you're still spending a pretty penny for that portrait each year. You can save yourself the money you would normally spend on a professional photographer by taking a class in digital photography. This way, for a one-time fee, you will learn what you need to know to get a well-lit, well-composed picture of your loved ones, and you'll be able to do it yourself for years to come.

Anything Pet-Related

Every dog owner should be having her dog groomed on a regular basis. Sure, I can bathe my dog when he gets dirty, but when he needs a haircut or his nails trimmed? I call the groomer. Though we let our dog's coat grow long in the winter so he can stay toasty on our long walks, during the warmer weather he gets groomed every two months or so. At $50 a pop, I'm easily spending $150 in dog grooming a year.

For $30, I could take an online course in dog grooming and learn how to take care of my pet without paying the groomer.

Or I could look into whether a nearby dog grooming school offers an "owner's" class or, better yet, discounted grooming if I let my dog be a test subject. (I know cosmetology schools do this with inexpensive haircuts on humans.) Another option is to see if any local technical schools may offer adult-education classes in dog grooming. If you have other kinds of pets, seek out similar learning experiences for how to groom them.

As far as dog training goes, you could sign up for a class at a store such as PetSmart, rather than hiring an expensive trainer to come to your house. Community colleges and local recreation departments may also have affordable classes related to pet ownership.

Business Know-How

Business skills related to the computer are always good to have—and you can find plenty of continuing education classes on them, as I did with the HTML class. But there are other areas of business where taking a class, which doesn't cost a lot up-front, may make a lot of sense for your financial and professional future. For example, a few years ago I took a free business plan–writing seminar through a local women-in-business organization. You may want to see if other kinds of specialized business groups near you offer similar classes. Here are some other areas where you can benefit from getting educated:

- Property management. If you invested in real estate as a way to earn extra income, you may have decided to hire an outside property management company to deal with the day-to-day needs of your tenants. These would include repairs, or a company that collects rent for you (for a fee). However, if you've got the time and inclination, you can save yourself from having to pay a third party to be your property manager if you learn to do it yourself.

- Construction project management. If you're getting ready to do a renovation on your home, this skill may allow you to avoid having to pay someone else to be your project manager, which can add to your total construction bill.
- Small-business ownership. If you're thinking about opening a small business or buying a franchise, a community college course can give you a leg up on getting into these kinds of business ventures. Organizations such as SCORE (*www.score.com*) offer pro bono help to would-be business owners.

Total Savings in This Chapter

Really, the sky's the limit when it comes to acquiring new skills that can save you money in the long run. In this chapter I offered suggestions on learning how to make your own cleaning products to save money as well as ways to dry clean clothing more cheaply. Not only do these cost-saving efforts really add up (I saved $360 a year by giving up my dry cleaning habit), they can make your clothes last longer, too. I estimate we've saved $500 in work clothes alone. In addition, learning to groom my own dog would save $120 annually.

Possible savings in Chapter 8:
$1,000
a year

chapter nine

RENOVATIONS AND INTERIOR DECORATING

If you're planning to renovate your current living space, you're in luck! You can find a treasure trove of frugal options if you think about ways to reuse what you already own or how to get stuff for free. This chapter provides a primer on how to make your home look its best for as little as possible. I'll delve into the world of renovations, and discuss when do-it-yourself trumps hiring a contractor—or vice versa. And I'll talk about inexpensive ways to make your home's décor shiny and new without spending much cash in the process.

Renovations

When it comes to improving your home's appearance, you need to think about your initial investment the same way that I did with that $200 L.L. Bean down coat (see page xi for a refresher on that anecdote). I could justify spending so much on a winter coat because I knew that it was a good investment over time.

You should think the same way when you approach a home renovation—spending a bit more on certain elements for your renovation can provide a bigger payback in the long run.

For example, if your kitchen needs a renovation, don't just do a half-baked job, using bargain-basement-quality cabinets and supplies—because in ten years you'll need to redo everything. When you settle for subpar materials, that low up-front spending decision is a proverbial penny-wise-and-pound-foolish one.

The truth is, a well-done kitchen renovation may provide you with your biggest return on investment of your time and money. What does that mean in plain English? When you sell your house, you will most likely recoup whatever money you put into that kitchen renovation with the increased value of your home overall—more so than a renovation in any other part of your home.

Get Cash for Your Old Appliances

Believe it or not, your old kitchen appliances may still have some value. When it comes time to get rid of them, don't just put them out by the curb as trash. See if you can sell them via Craigslist and make a couple of bucks. If that doesn't work, you could give them away on Freecycle. Even better than giving them away for free? Seeing if the company from which you're buying your new appliances will take away your old appliances to recycle them. Some stores even offer you a discount on the price of your new appliances because of the money they'll make on the back-end when they recycle your old stuff for scrap. Ask about this option.

According to BankRate.com, the financial website, the following home renovations provide the top five best returns on investment, in order of their potential payback:

- Kitchen remodel
- Bathroom renovation or addition
- Family room remodel or addition
- Bedroom addition
- Master suite renovation

In this section of the chapter, I'm focusing on lower-cost ways to get higher-payback renovations or improvements in these five biggest bang-for-your-buck areas of the house.

Kitchen

The first time my husband and I renovated a kitchen, we did everything wrong. We bought our cabinets through our local home improvement store, we paid a pricey designer to handle the layout of the kitchen and the creation of expensive countertops, and we allowed ourselves to be talked into fancy add-ons that we ended up not needing. When we sold our house, I'm sure that the great-looking kitchen helped us get a fair price for our home, but I've got a feeling that we probably could have cut our kitchen remodel budget in half and still recouped our investment by selling our house at the same price.

In our new house, we're planning to renovate the kitchen as well—it's in dire need! This time, though, we're planning on investing in high-quality products while keeping our frugal principles in mind. Here are five ways we're going to do that—and you can, too:

1. Reuse some of the existing kitchen cabinetry. Not every drawer, door, or cabinet in our circa 1961 kitchen is worth saving—or can be saved. But there are a number of pieces that it would be criminal to take off and toss out. That's why we'll carefully consider which cabinets we can sand, paint, and refinish in lieu of buying new ones, and which ones we have no choice but to put out as a "curb alert" on Freecycle or Craigslist. By reusing at least some of the existing cabinets, we should be able to shave a few hundred dollars off of our total cabinet bill.
2. Use our contractor to get wholesale prices on cabinets and countertops. If you're using a contractor to renovate your home, including your kitchen, he may be able to get you into so-called remodeling private clubs where you can buy kitchen cabinetry and other supplies at wholesale prices. The contractor doesn't even need to go with you—he can write you a note, which you can take with you and show the employees there. Once you've got that "in," you can pick out what you need for your kitchen and have it delivered to your home—at the price that contractors get. Or ask your contractor how much he would charge if he got the supplies and you install them on your own. This could save you the contractor's markup, assuming you feel qualified to install your own kitchen cabinets. (Perhaps look into the DIY clinics at Lowe's or Home Depot that I mentioned on page 131.)

   If you don't have a contractor or builder, you can always get a visitor's pass to Direct Buy (*www.directbuy.com*). This warehouse club–like, membership-only store promotes itself as a place to buy home remodeling supplies as well as home furnishings at wholesale prices. It's worth a look around.

3. Don't change your kitchen layout too much. It's when you start taking down walls and putting up new ones, or moving your sink from one side of the room to the other—and therefore have to reroute your plumbing—that the dollars start to add up on a kitchen renovation. If you keep the basic footprint, including the plumbing, like we're planning to do with our kitchen remodel, you should be able to keep your costs down.
4. Troll free and low-cost sources for supplies. It can be hit or miss when you have to rely on Freecycle or Craigslist for your new kitchen appliances or renovation supplies, but you may just get lucky and find exactly what you need for your kitchen. Case in point: recently I used Freecycle to give away a bunch of tile we couldn't use that I'd found in our basement. The person who took it from me could have conceivably used it for a kitchen backsplash. In addition, if there are any appliance clearance centers near you, check them out before buying retail. These could be the clearance center of a traditional retail store or the manufacturer itself. (A quick search of that manufacturer's website can help you figure out if there is a clearance center near where you live.)
5. Mix and match cabinet hardware. Whoever said that the drawer pulls and cabinet knobs had to match perfectly? Unless you're obsessive-compulsive, you could probably get away with searching the clearance bins at home-improvement stores and finding assorted pieces of cabinet hardware that complement each other, if they don't exactly match, to save money.

SEAL OF APPROVAL *HABITAT FOR HUMANITY RESTORE*

Habitat for Humanity ReStore stores (*www.habitat.org/env/restores.aspx*) are a mix between a home-remodeling warehouse and a thrift store. ReStores are where builders offload their overruns from construction projects (they get a tax write-off), and people donate used furniture and appliances. As with most thrift environments, you've got to sort through a lot of junk to find the jewels, but, trust me, this will be time well spent.

Recently, my husband was able to pick up two still-in-the-box Kohler bathroom sinks for our renovation. He paid $40 for both sinks at ReStore. When he saw the same sinks at a retailer, they were about $100 each.

I almost wished that we were ready to buy new kitchen appliances during that ReStore trip: there was a Sub-Zero refrigerator on sale at ReStore for $500; those babies go for ten times that (or about $5,000) at retail. Additionally, there was a KitchenAid stainless steel dishwasher for $225, compared to similar models, new at retail, selling for $800.

I've seen pictures on some ReStore websites of entire kitchen setups—cabinets, appliances, and countertops—that looked brand new and as if they were lifted right from a model home. Maybe they were. But I'd be willing to bet that at ReStore, those kitchen essentials would cost significantly less than what you'd pay for them in a model home or even a regular home-improvement store. Best of all, when you get your remodeling or renovation supplies at ReStore, you're supporting a good cause. That's why I'm giving a Suddenly Frugal Seal of Approval to Habitat for Humanity ReStore.

Bathroom Addition or Remodel

Our bathrooms, circa 1961 like the kitchen, also need to be remodeled. And as with our kitchen remodel, we're going to make these projects affordable by buying supplies as cheaply as possible—namely through the aforementioned Habitat for Humanity ReStore store.

DIY Demo

A great way to save money on any renovation, remodel, or addition is to do some of the prep work and demolition before the contractors arrive. Getting a new carpet installed? Spend the afternoon ripping up the old stuff yourself, and you could save a few hundred dollars on the installation costs. Redoing your bathroom? If you promise to rip out all of the old tiles, take down the drywall, and remove the old tub, leaving the room stripped down to the studs, your bathroom contractor will probably shave quite a bit off his price. Think about other ways that you can prep an area you're about to remodel in a way that will make less work for your contractor and more savings for yourself. Just remember to figure out how you'll dispose of the materials, since many contractors build the cost of disposal into their prices. For example, can you get rid of the construction debris through your trash hauler? The company I use gives each customer the opportunity, once a month, to put large, bulky items in the trash, and they don't charge extra to take those items away. Since you might be getting this service for free through the fee you already pay the trash hauler, this can keep your construction costs down.

Family Room Remodel or Addition

Perhaps the easiest way you can create a family room in a home that doesn't already have one is to finish your basement.

This is a good idea if you have younger children who have a treasure trove of toys, and you'd rather not see them—or worse, be stepping over them—on a daily basis.

Here's another way to look at a family room addition: are there rooms you currently have in your home that are being used in a certain, traditional way, but which you are actually not using on a regular basis? I'm thinking of homes that have formal living rooms that, frankly, are like a room in a museum. They always look perfect yet no one ever sits in them. Could you reclaim that space as a family room, without spending a dime in the process? Something to think about.

Bedroom Addition

While the most popular home layout overall in America continues to be a three-bedroom, two-bath home, where I live it's four bedrooms and up. In fact, most new homes being built are four bedroom, two-and-a-half bath abodes. So if you're thinking of adding a bedroom, you would probably get more out of putting a third bedroom onto a two-bedroom house, or a fourth bedroom onto a three-bedroom home. After that I can't imagine that the returns are worth the construction investment.

Also, keep this in mind when considering adding another bedroom: if you have to capture space from surrounding rooms in order to eke out that additional bedroom—thus making all of the rooms smaller overall—your renovation may come back to bite you in the long run. No one wants a house with lots of little rooms in it. Many Realtors I've spoken to say that a home with fewer but bigger rooms is more attractive than a home with five postage stamp–sized bedrooms.

If you want to add a bedroom, think about getting it one of these ways:

- Actually adding on to your home.
- Remodeling your basement to include a bedroom (could be your guest room).
- Converting your attic space into a bedroom, if that's possible. (Bankrate says that a bedroom addition of this type usually gives you an 82 percent return on investment.)

Master Suite Renovation

When we were selling our old home, here was the most consistent criticism we got about our master bedroom: it wasn't big enough, and it didn't have a sitting room. Now, to me that criticism was ludicrous. The master bedroom was plenty big, with a walk-in closet and attached master bath. It featured high ceilings, hardwood floors, and lots of built-ins. To me it was a perfectly functional master bedroom, and I couldn't understand what all the fuss was about—and why people were disappointed in the bedroom scenario and therefore not making an offer. Then I discovered that in the houses that were for sale at the same time in my neighborhood and in nearby subdivisions, the master bedrooms really were master suites. There was a nook off the bedroom that people had turned into a sitting room or a small home office, and the master bathroom was all jazzed up, too, with soaking tubs or Jacuzzis, and other spa-like accessories in the room.

If I could do that home sale over again, here are the kinds of renovations I might have done:

- Capture some of the space of the walk-in closet to carve out an actual sitting nook.
- Invest in higher-end bathroom fixtures to make the master bath seem more spa-like.

- Rearrange the master bedroom layout to create the appearance of a sitting nook.

If you're looking to renovate your master bedroom, think about some of these more affordable options that can improve the appearance of the master suite—and provide a greater return on your investment. Even something as simple as putting new doors on the master bedroom can help. I've seen some houses that went from a single-door entrance to a double-door setup, which made the whole space seem grander off the bat.

Redecorating

The cheapest way you can improve how your home looks is simply to redecorate it with items you already own or by just changing up the décor with a few well-placed (and new) accessories. Also, don't discount the value of a fresh coat of paint. It might just be the best $30 or so you spend spiffing up a room.

Here are some more ways to bring these and other redecorating ideas to life on a frugal budget.

Choosing Home Décor That's More than Just Pretty

When we were shopping for drapes in my old home, we ended up spending a bit more on window coverings than we'd originally planned. However, rather than feeling buyer's remorse, I was elated. Why? Because I knew that our investment in window treatments would pay off in the long run. Here's why.

We chose to buy insulated drapes (I got them from the Solutions catalog: *www.solutions.com*) that would help us manage our energy usage. We made this decision because we had rooms with big windows where I knew a lot of cold air escaped in winter and, when the sun was beating down on our house during summer, the windows allowed our home to heat up. I could close or open the drapes as necessary, and that allowed me to lower my heating and cooling bills over time.

Reuse What You Already Own

Why not try rearranging furniture or moving items to different rooms? This will change how things look without spending a dime on new pieces. Or, reach inside your cabinets to drag out old wedding gifts, and display them anew on fireplace mantels, side tables, or bookshelves. Again, new looks for no money. You could also repaint some wooden furniture or reupholster some dining room chairs—these kinds of changes help you revamp a look without spending a lot of cash. (You can find some cool, cheap decorating ideas on the Fabulous & Frugal website: *www.fabandfru.com*.)

Purchase Small Accessories for Big Effect

Troll the clearance aisles at discount stores such as Marshalls and T.J. Maxx, or regular stores such as Target, for inexpensive, brightly colored accessories that give your room pop. Just adding a few new well-placed pillows on a couch or a jewel-toned vase in the corner of the room can make it look as if you redid the whole space when you only added a few new things.

Use Kids' Art as Decorations

If you have kids, you probably have a spot in your home piled high with kids' art projects. I know that I do and, over the years, I wasn't quite sure what to do with these "masterpieces," but I didn't want to throw them out. Instead of having these works of art collect dust where no one can see them, why not pick out a few choice pieces and use them to decorate your living spaces?

I recently discovered some still-life paintings my daughters did when they attended art camp. One daughter did a still life with turnips and the other a still life with cupcakes. And you know what? They're not half bad. So I put them both in frames (purchased on clearance for about a buck each at my favorite craft store), and now they're adorning the walls of our dining room. When I tire of them, I'll find two other pieces of their art to put into rotation.

Decorate like a Model Home

This is a trick that home stagers use when they want to dress up a home so that it will sell faster. They'll arrange a kitchen to look like a model home by setting a beautiful cookbook on an easel on the kitchen countertop, or putting a pile of gorgeous coffee table–style books on the, well, coffee table. One home stager I know suggests checking out the bargain book table at your local bookstore for a cookbook with a beautiful cover that has colors that coordinate with your décor. You can get more home-staging ideas here: *www.movinghomeinteriors.com.*

Dress Up Dollar Store Finds

If you change the way you look at items you find in the dollar store, you can uncover lots of clever products that can add to your home décor without breaking the bank. Look for things such as tea lights, fabric place mats, or even inexpensive towels to dress up a bathroom. One professional I spoke to suggested stapling bamboo place mats from the dollar store to the wall above a bed to create a faux headboard.

Total Savings in This Chapter

Many of the money-savings ideas I've offered in this chapter will come to fruition down the road for you, if you renovate and then recoup your investment when you sell your house. But perhaps the best takeaway advice from this chapter was my Suddenly Frugal Seal of Approval winner—the Habitat for Humanity ReStore. Just in the ReStore examples alone, I showed how you could save about $5,200 on appliances and supplies for a kitchen and bathroom renovation.

Possible savings in Chapter 9: $5,200

chapter ten

IN THE GARDEN AND AROUND THE YARD

If there's anything I've learned from my Yankee-raised mother, it's this: just because you're living frugally doesn't mean that you can't have great landscaping or a nice-looking yard. When I was a child and we didn't have a lot of money, my mother always found ways to keep our yard and gardens looking like a million bucks. This chapter discusses how you can go green (as in your garden) without spending a lot of green. It also uncovers landscaping ideas that offer optimal energy savings, such as lowered heating and cooling bills, as well as plants that won't make your water bill go through the roof.

I'll admit that much of this chapter's advice is applicable only to homeowners, and I know that it wasn't until my husband and I bought our house that we fully appreciated the notion of DIY gardens. That's because after using our life savings on the home's down payment, we didn't have any money left over to hire a landscaper or a gardener—especially since, according to the National Gardening Association (NGA), the average American household spends about $1,295 annually on hired landscaping services. Um, yeah, we definitely didn't have that kind of money to spend.

At the same time we weren't going to live without some kind of garden. What was important to us was getting the most bang for our gardening buck by making smart choices about which plants we put in. We really didn't want to see our hard-earned dollars wither and die in the front yard. According to the NGA, American households spend about $405 per year on DIY gardening. While that was a way better number than the $1,295 to hire someone to plant our garden, I still wanted to spend a little less than the national average to do our own landscaping, or if we did end up spending that much, I wanted to make sure I had something to show in my garden for every dime I'd spent.

Following are some of the ways you can make smart-and-savvy gardening decisions, with the idea of spending as little as possible to get your gardens planted.

Climate-Controlled Gardening

The most basic tip in frugal gardening is to figure out what you can plant that will require the least amount of effort, investment, and, if you pay for your water and sewer services, water to keep your garden and yard plantings alive. Here are two ways to do that.

Plant Perennials

As far as effort goes, stick with perennial plants in your garden rather than annuals. Perennials are those that come back each year, such as the daffodils in spring and the mums in fall. Annuals are plants you put in the ground or in a pot once, you enjoy them while they're still vibrant, and then they die, never to be seen again. Some annuals you might be familiar with are petunias and geraniums.

Heat and Cool Your Home with . . . Trees?

Yes! If you've got shade trees planted on your property, you know how they can help keep your house cool in the summer and warm in the winter. If you don't have shade trees and you're looking to redo your landscaping, then think about planting some deciduous trees (those that lose their leaves) on the southern and eastern sides of your home—the sides that get the most sunlight during the days. During summer, when they have their leaves on, they create a natural canopy of shade. Then in winter, when the leaves are gone, they have wide-open spaces for the sun to stream through and warm your house.

That's why perennials trump annuals when living frugally—you only have to pay for these plants once. The best part about getting your garden established with perennials is that after a few years, you can split your plants and move them around the yard. This allows you to freshen up the garden without spending money on new plants—kind of like decorating your home with items you already own and have just moved to a different spot in the house (as I suggested in Chapter 9, "Renovations and Interior Decorating").

Use "Native" Plants

When choosing plants for your garden, pick species and varieties that are "native" to where you live, or at least those that are known to thrive in your climate. You want to think this way because native plants are low maintenance (you won't have to struggle to keep them alive because they are at home in your soil), and they won't need additional watering beyond normal rainfall in your area.

Here's another benefit to choosing native plants: as with local fruits and veggies, if your plants come from a farm nearby, they should be more affordable than plants that may have been grown in hothouses in South America and shipped to a store nursery.

For more information on native species, you can visit your state's cooperative extension website (once again, a great resource), or the website of the United States Forest Service (*www.fs.fed.us*).

Watering Your Garden

Ideally, you're planting a garden or landscaping your yard in a way that uses as little water as possible. But I understand that there are occasions when you do need to water your plants, as I do when I keep pots of seasonal flowers on my front step. Since these plants are baking in the sun all day, they get pretty thirsty on a regular basis. Here's one simple frugal watering tip: always water early in the morning or late in the day. Basically, don't water during the heat of the day, when more of your water will evaporate rather than drench your soil.

Then there's this issue: Why pay for water when you can find free water to use instead?

Free Ways to Water Your Garden

I'll bet it doesn't surprise you that I like to figure out ways to water my plants for free. Here are some of those ways, which might work for you, too.

- Use dehumidifier water. Since I run my dehumidifier in the summer to help keep my house cool, I need to empty its water receptacle frequently. When it's full, I'll use that to water my indoor plants or the garden outside.
- Employ a rain barrel. The smartest way to get your free water from nature is simply to set up a rain barrel outside. You can hook the barrel into your gutter system, so that any runoff goes right into it. Then, when you need to water the plants, you've got your water supply at the ready. You can also create a rain barrel–like setup for sump-pump water runoff. Instead of just pumping it into the street or sewer, feed it into your rain barrel.
- Empty leftover water bottles and cups. Walk around my home on any given day, and you'll find many cups and reusable water bottles that are still half full of water sitting on counters, tables, or in the sink. (Note to self: Get family to do a better job of bussing their cups.) Whenever I find one of these cups or bottles, here's what I do: rather than just dumping its water down the drain before loading it into the dishwasher, I'll use this extra water to give the plants a drink.
- Create a makeshift graywater system. Graywater is defined as "waste water," the stuff that you can reuse but you can't drink or cook with, such as the water from my dehumidifier. Here's another way to get and use graywater around the house: plug up the tub when you take a shower, then use the water that collects from your washing and rinsing off to water your plants. According to the North Carolina Cooperative Extension Office, you don't want to use overly soapy water on plants, as it might harm them. So plug the tub after you've shampooed, since it's likely to create the most soap bubbles, and then reuse the remaining water on the plants.

Getting Gardening Tools for Free or Close to It

When my husband was building a swing set in the backyard of our old house, he needed an auger in order to dig down far enough in the ground to secure the structure. Rather than pay money for one, he borrowed an auger from a neighbor.

I'm sure there were plenty of times during your spendthrift days that, when you needed a landscaping tool, you would just head out to your local home-improvement store to buy one. No more! Rather than spend your hard-earned cash buying new, why not get your gardening tools for free—or close to it—in one of the following ways.

- Borrow from a friend, neighbor, or family member.
- Borrow using an established network, such as Freecycle (*www.freecycle.org*), neighBORROW (*www.neighborrow.com*), or Ziloks (actually a rental service but super-affordable, at *http://us.zilok.com*).
- Peruse yard and garage sales for used tools, or look on Craigslist. Granted, you'll have to pay something for tools you acquire this way, but I'm sure you'll pay a lot less than you would if you were paying retail.

Starting a New Garden for (Practically) Free

Usually when you want to start a new garden, you have to identify the area where you want to make the garden, mark it off, and then fill it with topsoil so you have something to plant in. Unless you're getting bags of topsoil for free from Freecycle (possible; see the section in the next chapter on Freecycle), chances are you're spending money on those bags of dirt. What if I told you that you could start a new garden for free, without spending a dime on dirt?

Try Lasagna Gardening

This is exactly what I did last year when I decided to get a garden going in my front yard. Thanks to a comment on my Suddenly Frugal blog, I gave something called lasagna gardening a try. Here's what the commenter wrote about the concept: "Instead of digging a garden, you build one by layering leaves, grass clippings, compost, dirt, etc. on top of layers of newspaper or cardboard."

I was intrigued, because this sounded relatively easy. Also, because my front yard is currently covered in ground cover—myrtle and ivy—I wasn't looking forward to the task of digging all of that up to start a new garden bed. (Have you ever attempted to deal with the roots of a ground-cover plant? They're endless and annoying.)

Here's another reason I felt confident I could make lasagna gardening work for me: I had been "making" compost with leftover food scraps, coffee grounds, and shredded paper for more than a year but hadn't been able to do anything with the resulting soil. This seemed like the perfect opportunity.

Let me tell you exactly how I went about making my lasagna garden for free, and how you can, too. First, though, you'll need the following to get going:

- Newspapers or flattened sheets of cardboard
- Leaves or grass clippings
- Compost material, either from your own composter or lots of coffee grounds that you've been collecting. (By the way, you can ask your local Starbucks about taking their coffee grounds off their hands; the company's "Grounds for Your

Garden" program gives out free coffee grounds to inquiring customers. You can get more details on the Starbucks website: *www.starbucks.com.*)

Now, the six steps to make a lasagna garden:

❶ Lay down layers of newspaper to choke out any grass or weeds below. Put at least three layers of newspaper down, and then wet the sheets so they don't blow away. (Note: don't lasagna garden on a windy day or you'll be chasing newspapers all over your yard.) Wetting the newspapers also helps to kick-start the decomposition process. So it's practical and proactive!

❷ Put down a layer of leaves or grass clippings (if you have them) on top of the newspaper. By the way, if you compost, you know that in order to get your organic matter to break down, you need to layer it brown, green, brown, green, etc. The lasagna garden, which is really a composting garden, is no different. So the first layer of leaves or grass clippings is your first layer of brown, even though they're green. Stick with me on this, okay?

❸ Spread your "green" layer, which in this instance is probably brown, because it's your compost material or coffee grounds. Try to make this layer twice as thick as the "brown" layer. It will make for richer soil. (For a composting primer, please turn to page 160.)

❹ Put another layer of "brown" (leaves or grass clippings) down.

❺ Add your last layer of "green."

❻ Top off the pile with a final covering of leaves or grass clippings.

I was told that a lasagna garden is supposed to be close to two feet high when you're done, but mine ended up being about sixteen inches high. I'm thinking that size doesn't matter in this case because when spring rolled around, I had an awesome six-foot-by-six-foot gardening bed that was ready-made for new plants. Best of all, it didn't cost anything to make, and it didn't kill my back to dig down into it when I finally did put some plants in it. The soil was like butter.

Get Free Stuff for Your Garden

There's way more free stuff to be had for your garden than using your compost, old newspapers, and grass clippings to make a new bed. Here are some of the ways that you can stock your garden without spending a dime:

- Request stuff on Freecycle or Craigslist. A "Wanted" ad on Freecycle last year resulted in my getting four tiger lily plants, one lilac bush, one Rose-of-Sharon tree, one Saint John's wort shrub, and my composting bin.
- Swap plants with gardeners you know. After a few years most plants need to be thinned, which you can accomplish by splitting them. So the next time you split your hostas or mums, offer to share these plants with others who can use them. Likewise, ask those you know who enjoy gardening if they'll do the same for you with plants you don't currently have in your garden. To find other like-minded gardeners near you, check out the gardening forums on iVillage (*http://forums.gardenweb.com/forums/exchind*).
- Don't be embarrassed to dumpster dive. Well, dragging plants out of the garbage is more likely than actually diving into a dumpster. But seriously, I can't tell you how many people I see putting perfectly good potted plants out at the

curb on trash or leaf collection day. Last fall, I grabbed what looked to be a potted gardenia tree from outside a house at the end of my street. That tree happily basked in the sun in our family room all winter long, and "rewarded" us with fragrant, white gardenia blooms in the spring. I found out that, bought at retail, gardenia trees cost about $50. I love that I got mine for free.

Composting Primer

The chore that many kids have (and dread) when they're growing up is taking out the trash. When I was a kid, I had to take out the compost. For as long as I can remember, my mother was composting our food scraps. She didn't have a fancy composting bin in our yard, just a pile behind the woodpile and the shed. This is where, on a regular basis, I dumped whatever peels, rinds, and bread heels we'd toss in the compost bucket that we kept in the sink.

Like mother, like daughter, right? Because when I grew up and got my own house, I started composting, too. Here's what you need to know to get started.

- You can throw just about any organic matter in your compost—vegetable peels, apple cores, seeds, popcorn, coffee grounds, eggshells, and more. You can even put paper towels ripped into little pieces, tissues, dryer lint, dog hair, and shredded office paper in the compost—even those little pink packets that artificial sweetener comes in. Here's what you can't put in the compost: dairy, meat, and bones. These three items tend to attract animals, and they can smell really bad.

- You will actually have two compost receptacles. One will be a small bucket that you'll keep in the house for collecting food scraps as you cook or clean up. (I keep my bucket under the sink; my mother keeps hers in the sink; another friend uses a mini flip-top trashcan that she keeps on the countertop next to the sink.) The other receptacle is your actual composting bin, which you keep outside. When the inside bucket is full, bring it outside and dump the contents into the compost bin. Every time you dump "green" matter (i.e., your organic matter described above), you need to cover it with a thin layer of "brown" matter. "Brown" could be dried leaves, mulch, or grass clippings. (I tend to use dried leaves, which are plentiful and free in my shaded yard.)
- Every week or so, you should turn your compost. You can use a pitchfork for this. The idea is to get the air circulating so that everything can break down into soil. If when turning the compost you notice that things are sticky and wet, add some shredded paper to the compost bin. This will help to absorb the extra moisture. Trust me—you don't want that extra moisture in there. It can make your compost smell bad, and too much moisture can slow down the biodegrading process.
- Because composting works with heat, your compost will decompose and turn to dirt faster in warmer weather. During the winter, you won't see much happening. It's as if your compost is hibernating. Just wait out the winter, and as soon as the weather warms again, the compost pile will start getting smaller as everything starts to break down again. This heat thing is another reason that most composting bins are black (to absorb the sun's heat) and why some people believe it's a good idea to keep your compost bin in the sun. I tried that last year, and all the sun did was heat up the contents so I had the wafting smell of warm garbage in my yard. This past year, after

using up my compost supplies in the aforementioned lasagna garden, I moved the bin to a shadier spot. It gets sun only late in the day, and so far it doesn't smell as much, and everything still seems to be breaking down into dirt on schedule.

SEAL OF APPROVAL *COMPOSTING*

While most people think of composting as something green to do, composting also makes sense if you're looking to live frugally. Just look at the section on page 157 about how I used my compost to make a garden. Thanks to my dedication to composting rather than throwing away used food, I was able to save money by not having to buy topsoil for a new garden.

In addition, composting has saved me money in another way—with my trash service. If you pay for trash pickup by the bag, you'll definitely see a savings. I can get away with paying for once-a-week service (most people in my area get their trash picked up twice a week). By taking food scraps out of the trash equation, I have significantly decreased what we throw out as garbage. Before we started composting, I was probably emptying our trashcan a minimum of four times a week or about every other day. These days, the only time I have to actively empty the trash is when I cook chicken, and I don't want the scraps to rot and stink up the house. I've also saved money by not having to buy garbage bags as frequently. These are all the reasons why I'm giving a Suddenly Frugal Seal of Approval to composting.

Deer and Your Garden

When we first started thinking about our garden, we thought our clay-laden soil would be our biggest problem with getting a garden going. However, we quickly realized that there were bigger issues looming in the woods: deer.

Like many suburban subdivisions, our neighborhood had encroached on a deer pack's natural habitat. This was problematic for a number of reasons. There were frequent deer-car collisions, cases of Lyme disease were on the rise, and the deer were treating our gardens as all-you-can-eat buffets that were open 24/7. It was like the Old Country Buffet in my front yard for deer!

After my mother generously shared hosta plants from her own garden to get ours started, we discovered that hostas were deer salad. Each morning we would find most of our hostas nibbled down to a stub. Soon enough our thinly planted garden of hostas was reduced to nothing. Granted, we hadn't paid for these plants so we hadn't actually lost any money on them. But now we had to go out and buy new plants to replace the hostas, and this caused our landscaping budget to go into the red.

Before we hit the stores, though, we decided to do some research on deer-proof plants. I mean, if I was going to spend my hard-earned money on plants and then do the digging to get them into the ground, I didn't want the deer showing up that night to eat everything. The most frugal thing we could do would be to plant a garden that would, as much as possible, repel the deer.

Here are two things I learned from that experience:

1. Your local state university's co-op extension program is a fabulous, free resource for determining which plants are deer-proof in your state as well as which plants are appropriate for your climate and topography.
2. When deer are really hungry and it's been a harsh winter, they will eat just about anything.

As far as the first point goes, my husband and I used the Penn State Co-op Extension's website to find out which plants fared the best in our Pennsylvania climate as well as those that repel deer. At first we couldn't find the deer-proof or deer-resistant information we were searching for, and so my mom recommended the Cornell University's Co-op Extension website to find out which plants the deer don't like. This was the website she'd used when planting her garden in the New York home where I grew up.

Here's what we discovered after we took some of the suggestions off the Cornell site and planted them—New York deer and Pennsylvania deer do not have the same taste in plants. Whereas the Cornell website had recommended phlox, for example, as a deer-resistant plant, the deer in my neighborhood loved it. They ate it up, literally. Who knew that deer had regional taste buds?

We soon realized that if we were going to figure out how to plant a deer-resistant garden, we were going to have to rely on hyper-local resources, such as the guys at our local gardening center as well as the co-op extension office in our *county*, not just our state. (By the way, the purple butterfly bush, yellow coreopsis, and blue-flowered myrtle ground cover that we eventually planted in place of the phlox and hosta all flourished.)

Now on to the second point, about how the deer are hungry enough to eat anything when conditions are bad. We had a couple of very harsh winters after we'd planted our now deer-resistant garden—winters with early frosts and late snowfalls, and not a lot of naturally occurring vegetation in between. During the years like this when the deer were starving, there just wasn't anything that we could do about the hungry deer eating our plants. My neighbors tried everything from buying and spraying coyote urine on their plants (didn't work) to covering them with netting (deer ate right through it. Probably wasn't the best for the deer's digestive tract, but I don't think my neighbors cared).

I realize that deer might not be a problem where you live—heck, it could be the bunnies that wreak havoc on your garden. But I would still highly recommend a cooperative extension office as a gardening resource. In fact, though the Cornell University Cooperative Extension website originally steered us toward the wrong deer-resistant plants for our Pennsylvania garden (which was not Cornell's fault), I've since found a page on that site that includes links to deer-resistant information of all kinds for different states (*www.hort.cornell.edu/gardening/factsheets/deerdef/*). It even tells you where you can buy "predator urine" if you're interested. Based on my neighbor's experience with coyote urine, I say save your money. Maybe you could send your boys outside to pee on the plants for free instead.

Growing Your Own Food

Perhaps you're interested in learning how to grow your own food. Well, you wouldn't be alone in that interest. According to a 2009 NGA survey, food gardening in the United States is on the rise: this survey showed that as many as 7 million more households plan to grow their own fruits, vegetables, herbs, or berries these days. There are three reasons most folks are interested in gardening—and maybe why you are, too: higher-quality food, better-tasting food, and smaller grocery bills. This last point is probably what you're after, and I've got good news on that front. According to the NGA, a well-maintained food garden can slice as much as $500 off your annual grocery bill.

Luckily, it doesn't take a PhD in horticulture to start your own produce garden. All you need is a sunny spot in your yard (or on your balcony or porch, if you don't have a yard) and some fertile ground. This is a great time to dig into your compost supplies and use them in the dirt where you plant your produce garden.

If you'd like to start your garden from seeds, you can get your gardening going over the winter by turning used toilet paper rolls into seed-starting cups (see more about this on page 209). People also use cardboard egg cartons in the same way. What's great is that you can plant all of this right into the ground come spring, because the cardboard is biodegradable.

I like to take a more haphazard approach to gardening with seeds. Basically, rather than dealing with store-bought seeds, I'll take the guts out of certain fruits and vegetables, burying them under whatever compost matter I'm using in my vegetable garden, and then see what time brings as things start to grow.

A few years ago we became what I call "accidental" pumpkin gardeners because of my method. That's because we'd dumped into our garden the innards of a pumpkin that we'd carved out for a Halloween jack-o'-lantern. Come fall we had pumpkin vines taking over our yard. We had enough pumpkins for that year's Halloween without having to go out and buy any—saving us at least $30 in the process. And as long as we continued to do the dump-and-run with seeds and guts in the fall, we'd always have enough pumpkins for our Halloween the next year. I've heard of others who've used this approach to grow cantaloupes, cucumbers, and peppers.

For more on getting an edible gardening off the ground—or rather into the ground—I recommend a book that my friend Daria "Dee Dee" Bowman wrote: *The Complete Idiot's Guide to Vegetable Gardening* (Alpha Books, 2009). Or, try *The Everything® Grow Your Own Vegetables Book*. Both are excellent resources.

Total Savings in This Chapter

You wouldn't think that your garden or lawn, or even a compost pile, could save you a bunch of money, but I hope that this chapter has changed your mind. Thanks to all of the suggestions in the preceding pages, you can avoid hiring a landscaping service (to save $1,295 a year), cut your grocery bill by growing your own vegetables (to save $500 a year), and cut down on the costs of your trash service (to save $40 a year like we did.)

Possible savings in Chapter 10:
$2,000
a year

chapter eleven

GETTING SOMETHING FOR (ALMOST) NOTHING

In our consumer-centric society, shopping has become second nature for most Americans. But you don't always have to shop in first-rate stores and pay first-rate prices when you need something. In this chapter I will help open your eyes to the many places, both offline and online, where you can find something for nothing—or almost nothing. You'll learn how to find the ultimate frugal bargains on nearly anything you need for your day-to-day life, whether it be entertainment you swap for or little gadgets around the house that you can turn into useful tools. As my husband likes to say, "Free—that's my favorite price."

SEAL OF APPROVAL *FREECYCLE*

One of the first and best places to get something for nothing is Freecycle (*www.freecycle.org*). Heck, it's even got "free" in its name. As I write in Chapter 10, "In the Garden and Around the Yard," Freecycle has helped me to get so much stuff for my home for just the cost of driving somewhere to pick it up, including free plants and shrubs for my garden as well as a compost bin.

The cool thing about Freecycle is that you can use it proactively to both give away and receive items. Case in point: when we moved into our new house a few years ago, we brought with us kid-oriented furniture that we'd had in our old playroom. Once we got here and started to arrange and furnish our new playroom, we realized that things such as the two bright purple desks that my daughters had loved when they were little no longer worked in the playroom. These desks were still perfectly good for someone else with younger kids so I put them up as an "Offer" on my local Freecycle group.

Conversely, when I wanted to plant my garden or start composting, I was able to use a "Wanted" ad on Freecycle to secure both items for free from a fellow Freecycle user.

If free really is a frugal person's favorite price, then Freecycle definitely has my Suddenly Frugal Seal of Approval.

Freecycle Basics

Maybe you're not familiar with Freecycle or its offshoot groups called RecycleIt or the ReUseIt Network (*www.reuseitnetwork.org*)—these splinter groups have various names around the country. That wouldn't surprise me, since a recent survey on my Suddenly Frugal blog uncovered this: six out of ten readers either had heard of Freecycle but never used it or didn't know what Freecycle was. The mission of Freecycle and other swapping groups is the same—to keep stuff out of landfills by passing it along to someone else. In the process, it lets others get items for their home, garden, or whatever for free.

First, let me explain how you find and join your local group, and then we'll get into the nitty-gritty of how Freecycle works—and how it can benefit your frugal budget.

Joining Freecycle

If you'd like to take advantage of the giveaways on Freecycle, the first thing you need to do is join your local group. Most of these are run through either Yahoo Groups (*http://groups.yahoo.com*) or Google Groups (*http://groups.google.com*). You usually need to get the group leader's blessing in order to join. When you try to join one of these groups, this leader gets an automatic e-mail request, and once she approves you, you're in.

To find the local groups, you can visit The Freecycle Network's home page at *www.freecycle.org* and find a location near you. (The website says there are more than 4,700 groups worldwide.) Or you can search using your location and the word "Freecycle" via your favorite search engine. Not only will this uncover the actual Freecycle groups near you, but you'll likely also find out about, as I mentioned earlier, the offshoot groups that former Freecycler members have formed. They may have names like ReUseIt, RecycleIt, or Meetup (*www.meetup.com*). In Canada, they're called FullCircles (*www.fullcircles.org*). In addition, there are a number of city-specific groups that focus on reusing items and keeping them out of landfills but they have nothing to do with Freecycle. Two such examples are TwinCitiesFreeMarket.org in Minnesota and RedStickFreeUse (*www.redstickfree.org*) in Baton Rouge.

Be creative about how you search for groups near you. For example, I happen to live on the border of Pennsylvania and New Jersey. When I was looking to join my local Freecycle groups, I searched not only for groups in my county and state but also for groups in the county and state across the Delaware River from me. My mother lives in a rural area of Maine, so she joined all the Freecycle groups within a fifty-mile radius of her home. Using the previous Twin Cities example, you could also add any monikers that your area uses to your search terms to uncover additional groups you might want to join. For example, when I search for a Freecycle group using the term "Silicon Valley," it brings me to a link for all of the Bay Area Freecycle-like groups.

I recommend joining more than one group to give you a greater reach. It helps when giving stuff away—more people will see your "Offer" ad—and it helps when you want to get something for free because you're exposed to more "Offer" ads overall.

Using Freecycle to Give and Receive

I find it easiest to visit the Freecycle group's home page on Yahoo Groups and post using the web form. However, most of these Freecycle lists have a designated e-mail address (usually at the bottom of the e-mails you receive) that you can "reply to" to post a message as well.

The protocol for posting an ad is usually as follows:

1. Start the subject with either "Offer" or "Wanted"—obviously, based on whether you're looking to give something away or if you're in need of something. (Note: many Freecycle lists have an unwritten rule that in order to post a "Wanted" message, you must have first posted an "Offer" ad.)
2. Give a brief description of the item you're offering, also in the subject line. When I was giving away the kids' desk, I just wrote "Purple Kids' Computer Desks."
3. Finish the subject line with the town where you live and/or your zip code. This makes it easier for people to figure out whether it's worth the trip to pick up your item.

4. In the body of the message, describe as best as you can what the item is, with measurements if possible, and its condition. If your group allows you to post photos, include them when putting up an "Offer" ad.
5. If you have any pickup requirements, be sure to include those in the body of your message. I've learned that saying something like "Items must be picked up by this Friday" encourages those who are really interested in your item to actually show up. Otherwise, some people like to go "window shopping" on Freecycle. Without pickup requirements to go by, these folks just respond to a bunch of "Offer" ads and then pick and choose which ones they'll actually follow through on.

Once your post goes live and you've found someone to take your stuff off your hands, some people take an extra step of reposting to the list by "replying" to their own ad. They leave the body of the ad untouched, but change the subject from "Offer" to "Pending" or "PPU" (which stands up for "please pick up."). Finally, when the item is actually gone, they'll post once more with "Taken" in the subject line.

Freecycle users are, for the most part, a pretty active bunch. If you post an "Offer" ad, you can expect to get replies via e-mail minutes after your "Offer" goes out on the list. Yes, just minutes, especially if you're giving away something that either has a perceived value (such as electronics) or is commonly requested on your list (such as moving boxes).

Freecycle Etiquette

Once the e-mails start flooding into your inbox, it's up to you how you decide to whom to give your item. At first I adopted the "first come, first served" approach, meaning that the first person who e-mailed me was the person I chose to pick up the item. However, I've since learned that though it's fair to give your item to one of the first few people who respond, it's better to work with the person who can get the item from you the soonest. While it's nice to give stuff away, and to keep it out of landfills, you don't want to have your life start revolving around pickup times with fellow Freecycle users.

There are other sorts of unwritten etiquette rules involving Freecycle as well—most of which have to do with when you're on the receiving end of an "Offer" ad or you've posted a "Wanted" ad and find someone who has what you need. Here are some of those common-courtesy expectations:

- People who use Freecycle are not your personal shoppers. When you respond to an "Offer" ad, it is your job as the interested party to work with the person who is giving the item away. Don't reply with, "Oh, I'm going out of town tomorrow; can you hold it for a week?" or "Gas is too expensive; can you meet me somewhere halfway?" That's just rude.
- Respect time limits and a commitment to pick up your item. This rule kind of goes along with the one above. Bottom line: You should be bending over backward to pick up posthaste any item you've expressed interest in. If you can't work within the time frame that the person has posted for an item, don't respond.
- There are no givebacks or returns. Have you heard the phrase *caveat emptor*? It means buyer beware. That saying applies perfectly to getting stuff for free. You get something, it's yours. You don't get a return policy or a warranty. And you've got to live with the outcome. For example, last year when I got free plants for my garden via a "Wanted" ad on Freecycle, I planted them and they all died. But was it the fault of the

person who gave me these plants? Nope. It was the risk I took in getting plants for free.

- Be nice in whatever dealings you have with people. You know that little thing called karma? I think that in situations like Freecycle, it really is important to keep karma in mind. You are doing something good for someone by giving them something for free—or taking something off their hands for free—and there's no reason to be high-maintenance about the transaction. Smile and say "Thank you," and I'm confident that karma will come back to reap her rewards on you in the near future.

Other Free Sites

Freecycle isn't the only free game in town. There are a number of other virtual places where you can swap goods with others. Some are free like Freecycle and require in-person pickups; others are done through the mail, with your only cost being shipping and handling.

Craigslist

While people think of Craigslist as a place to get a date, a job, or an apartment, there is a whole section devoted to the exchange of goods and services—and I mean in a legal way. Look for the "For Sale" section of your local Craigslist site, then find the "Free" subcategory. In addition, if you're looking to receive something you want or need, you can place a free ad under "Wanted" or, if you're willing to barter for it, you can put your ad in the "Barter" section. Finally, if you'd like to make a few bucks selling something of value or wouldn't mind spending some money on something you need, you can look in the various categories in "For Sale." These categories range from "Arts and Crafts" to "Tools."

Swap Sites

While you can find plenty of kids' items offered on Freecycle groups, it's not a guarantee. My list can go for days with nary a toy or tricycle put up for offer. Therefore, if you're a parent looking to outfit your child or stock a playroom for as little money as possible, check out swap sites such as Zwaggle (*www.zwaggle.com*). This site is geared specifically toward parents with kids of all ages.

On Zwaggle you can find baby bedding, books, musical instruments, and sporting goods. As with many swap sites—and even Freecycle, where you may have to give before you can receive—you list items that you're giving away in order to earn points, called "zoints" on Zwaggle. Once you reach a certain level of points, then you can use those points to shop for items that others are giving away.

Unlike Freecycle or Craigslist, there are rarely in-person pickups associated with a Zwaggle swap. You can go shopping for free on Zwaggle, but you have to pay shipping and handling to get the goods.

Item-Specific Swap Sites

While Zwaggle does have categories for books, music, and videos, some people prefer to do their swapping on sites that specialize in certain items. Here are a handful of them:

- Those interested in books can try PaperBackswap.com or Bookmooch.com for getting and giving books. (See Chapter 5 for more details.)

- If you're looking for other kinds of media, such as video games, music, and movies, try SwapTree.com and Bookins.com (this latter site limits swaps to books and DVDs only). (These are also discussed in Chapter 5.)
- In addition, there are, at this writing, twenty-five different U.S. cities with Freepeats groups, which are dedicated to passing along gently used baby items. (Wish I'd known about them when I was knee-deep in onesies!) Note: there is a $4.95 lifetime membership fee for Freepeats, but you can try out the site for two weeks for free.

As with Zwaggle, most of these sites have users paying for shipping and handling only. However, I've heard that many of these types of sites are going to start charging nominal membership fees in the near future.

Find Free Moving Boxes

Though you can give away or take ownership of moving boxes on Freecycle, your moving company may be able to help you recycle and swap your moving boxes once your move is over. Two such companies doing that are U-Haul (*www.uhaul.com/boxexchange*) and New York City mover Moishe's (*www.moishesboxexchange.com*).

Bartering

The notion of bartering seems downright medieval until you stop to think about the value of it. I remember when, about a decade ago, a graphic design company I'd hired in my corporate job made me a barter offer I couldn't refuse. They knew I was leaving my position to launch my freelance business, and they suggested that they could create custom stationery and business cards for me if I, in turn, would do some promotional writing for them once I was out on my own. Together, we figured out how much the stationery and business cards would cost, and I gave them the same value in writing services.

Additionally, a few years ago, at the hair salon where I've been getting my hair cut and highlighted forever, my stylist happened to mention that the salon was planning a fundraising cut-a-thon. They were excited about the event but overwhelmed by the notion of actually promoting it. So even though my head was covered in foils, I negotiated a barter deal: I would promote the event to the local media for them in exchange for a year's worth of hair services. Given that I get my hair done four times a year (at about $100 a pop), this worked out to be a pretty good deal for me.

It isn't just writers like me who can barter for goods and services. Many companies that are tight on cash have started bartering to make ends meet. Do you have a skill that you can offer someone in exchange for something you want or need? I know some women who recently worked out a cooking/mending barter deal. One of the women offered to cook a week's worth of meals in exchange for another woman mending and hemming her family's clothes. Together, they saved money and time on cooking and getting items tailored.

If you decide you'd like to get something for almost nothing via bartering, here are five tips to keep in mind.

1. Understand the value of a barter. When I negotiated my past barter deals, I found out first the scope of the writing project the company wanted. Then, by considering my hourly fee, I was able to suggest an equally valuable barter

so we each would benefit in the end. In addition, I believe that I've been successful in bartering because I can offer a service that others find valuable. I would guess that I could say the same about a website designer or computer programmer who was looking to barter. Bottom line: make sure you have a service to offer that is potentially as valuable as the service you're looking to receive, and when you do find someone to barter with, make sure you get the full value of the services you are offering.

2. Have a clear idea of what you need ahead of time. Business owners are frequently advised to come up with a thirty-second commercial or their "elevator pitch." It's no different when you're looking to barter. When you can come up with a concise description of what service you need and what service you can offer, you can tell your potential barter partner, in a sentence or two, what you had in mind.
3. Use creative means to identify potential barter partners. As with most things in business, networking and word-of-mouth recommendations usually pay off in the long run. If you belong to a networking organization, local chamber of commerce, or even a playgroup with other moms, let them know about your desire to barter. Don't know anyone locally with whom you can barter? Then check places such as Craigslist, which has an entire subsection, under "For Sale," for bartering, or Time Banks (*www.timebanks.org*). This latter group, run through local civic and philanthropic organizations, lets you deposit your bartering time, and then it's up to you to search through its database of barter offers to figure out how you'll withdraw your time to get someone else to barter for you in return.
4. Get it in writing. Even though no money will exchange hands with a barter, you still want to get your agreement

in writing. In addition to including the basics of who and what are involved, also spell out the value of the services and the time line over which it will be completed.

5. Understand the tax implications of bartering. Uh, I know—taxes, how boring. But here's why this is important: just because you're getting something for "free" doesn't let you off the tax hook, especially if you file as a small business using a Schedule C. Here's how the Internal Revenue Service (IRS) sees bartering (as posted on their website):

If you engage in barter transactions you may have tax responsibilities. You may be subject to liabilities for income tax, self-employment tax, employment tax, or excise tax. Your barter activities may result in ordinary business income, capital gains or capital losses, or you may have a nondeductible personal loss. Barter dollars or trade dollars are identical to real dollars for tax reporting. If you conduct any direct barter—barter for another's products or services—you will have to report the fair market value of the products or services you received on your tax return.

This potential tax implication is yet another reason to make sure you keep good records with bartering, and why you want to have your agreement in writing. Of course, ask your tax provider how he or she thinks you should handle any bartering done during the tax year.

Sign Up for Freebies

In our frugal economy, when people are shopping less, marketers will do just about anything to entice us back into the stores. Though giving out free products is nothing new, these days you can sign up for them online when you join a "test panel" or special group that a company has put together for its "loyal" customers. The trick is figuring out the parent company of your favorite products or finding a product-specific website where you can get your name on a mailing list for free products.

For example, Procter and Gamble, maker of everything from Venus razors to Tide detergent, has a female-focused website called VocalPoint (*www.vocalpoint.com*). Like many product-oriented sites, VocalPoint includes discussion boards, how-to articles, and plugs for its products. Once you register, you can take surveys and, in many cases, start getting free products sent to you. The company wants your feedback and for you to share good thoughts with your friends and family—called word-of-mouth marketing. Whatever it's called, it could add up to free stuff for you, which can help keep your shopping bills in check. (Full disclosure: I've done some freelance work for this website.)

Suddenly Frugal Freebies

Because of the popularity of freebies, I've started a regular feature on my blog (*www.suddenlyfrugal.com*) called Freebie Friday. Each Friday (not surprisingly), my blog posting focuses on freebies to be had in the next seven days. These have ranged from free food at restaurants to free movies. Subscribe to my blog so you don't miss any Freebie Friday posts!

There are also third-party websites that feature free products. The catch is that you're supposed to test them, and then write up your opinion of the product or take a survey. One such website is SheSpeaks (*www.shespeaks.com*). It often works with products in development, which allow you to be on the cutting edge of something about to come to market, or you can help tweak and improve a long-standing product. According to the SheSpeaks website, members get to sample "a variety of products, services, and content ranging from hair care to snacks, books, TV shows, makeup, and more!"

Bottom line: If there are products you currently use and like, check the packaging for a website address. Then log on to those sites to see if you can sign up to get those products for free.

Find Freebies Around the House

You might be surprised to discover that you probably already have plenty of "freebies" sitting around your home. Besides the "trash" that you can reuse in new and different ways (as I describe in Chapter 13, "Don't Throw It Out—Wear It Out"), you can uncover items that you forgot you owned and that can become your de facto freebies.

Toiletries

How many times have you or a family member stayed in a hotel and loaded up on the free bottles of shampoo, conditioner, and lotion, along with bars of soap? And what happened to those items when you returned home? If you're like me, those items are in one of two places: still floating around inside your various suitcases or sitting under your bathroom sink where you dumped them when you got back.

Now that we're thinking about free stuff, try reclaiming those hotel-supplied toiletries as some of your freebies. Doing so could save you from having to buy shampoo, conditioner, lotion, and soap for a couple of weeks, if not months. Here's how reclaiming those items worked for me—and could work for you, too.

As part of a recent New Year's resolution, I swore I was going to get the cabinets under my master bathroom sink organized. To get started, I located all of those sample-size bottles and soap bars that had been scattered about in that under-sink area. I divided them up into categories, and then placed them in category-specific plastic bins. (The shampoos went in one bin, the conditioner in another, and so forth.) I must have had at least fifteen bottles each of shampoo, lotion, and conditioner, and twenty or more bars of soap. I labeled each bin and slipped them back under my now-organized bathroom sink. Just by reclaiming those "freebies" allowed us to avoid buying hair conditioner for one month and shampoo for three months; as of this writing, the soap and lotion supplies are still going strong.

Reuse Those Plastic Bags

While I try to bring reusable shopping bags with me when I grocery shop, sometimes I end up with the plastic bag that the store gives me. Instead of throwing these bags away or recycling them through collection bins at my supermarket, I find ways to reuse them around the house. These ways include lining trashcans, transporting wet bathing suits, and picking up after my dog. I also use the plastic sleeve that my daily newspaper comes in or in which bread is packaged for dog duty. Bottom line: I never have to buy "pooper scooper" bags. Note: Clearly if you live in a state such as California, which mandates that you recycle these plastic bags, follow the law and skip my suggestions here. I'm all for frugal living but I'm *not* for breaking the law.

Office Supplies

Beside the pens and pencils that always seem to end up coming home with us from birthday parties, doctor's offices, or hotel rooms, there are other kinds of office supplies that we've turned into our own freebies over the years. These have included pads of paper from conferences, and letter openers or paper-clip holders from trade shows.

The next time you think you need another notepad or a new box of pens, I dare you to look around your home. I'll bet you can dig up a handful of office supplies that can hold you off from shopping for them for at least a couple of weeks.

In addition, I've discovered a number of items that started life as office supplies but can also serve as "freebies" in other ways around your home. I call these "random reusables."

RANDOM REUSABLES: BINDER CLIPS

Between the documents from my husband's job and the documents my clients send to me, we have dozens of binder clips of various sizes scattered throughout the house. (These are those clips with the two silver "handles" that you squeeze to open and them clamp down to hold a stack of paper together.) Over time I've figured out the following ways to reuse binder clips:

- To close bags of food. We fold down the bag and use the clips to keep the top closed so that the contents stay fresh. Why pay for a colorful clip in the store that says something like "chips" on it when I can use a binder clip for free?
- To keep a page in a cookbook open. I'll use two binder clips to hold back the pages of the cookbook so it doesn't close on me.
- To mark a spot in a book or my calendar. Binder clips make for excellent bookmarks, because if you drop the book, the

bookmark won't fall out. The only caveat? They don't work on Harry Potter–sized books, and if you've borrowed a book from the library, you probably shouldn't use the binder clip at all or you risk leaving an indent on the pages of a book that isn't yours to maim.

- To replace a key chain fob. You can attach your keys on the ring to the metal "handle" part of a binder clip. What's great about using a binder clip as a fob is that it will be easy to find in your purse—I would say that a binder clip has a unique "feel" to it, even at the bottom of your bag. Then, when you get home, you can clip your keys in a visible spot so you don't lose them.

RANDOM REUSABLES: RUBBER BANDS

Our biggest source of rubber bands these days is our daily newspaper. Our paper is delivered bound either in a plastic bag (on wet days) or with a rubber band. Given that we get a newspaper every day, that's a lot of rubber bands to accumulate in one year. That's why I've come up with these reusable options for rubber bands.

- Keep bags closed. Like the binder clips above, rubber bands work perfectly well to keep a bag closed and the contents from getting stale.
- Secure decorations on the porch or a fence. This past Fourth of July we wanted to put up a red, white, and blue bunting on our fence, and rubber bands were all I had on hand. So I create something like a slipknot with the rubber band through the bunting's grommet, then secured it to the fence.
- Organize a desk drawer. Take a handful of pencils, pens, or crayons, and keep them together with a rubber band. This

way you can keep related items together in a semi-organized fashion in a desk drawer.

- Wrap a present. Instead of wasting tape on wrapping a present, use two rubber bands. Put them on perpendicular to one another to close the wrapping paper. This is an especially helpful hint if you like to wrap in fabric since tape doesn't stick to fabric like it sticks to paper!
- Keep a door open. There are times when you need a door that closes automatically (such as a screen door) to stay open. If there isn't a mechanism on the door to let you lock it in the open position, you can wrap one end of a rubber band around the doorknob and the other end around another doorknob (if there's one nearby), a post, or a stairwell banister. The rubber band has just enough give to keep the door open without it snapping.
- Open a jar. If you have trouble opening a jar, put a rubber band around the lid, then twist off the lid. The rubber band provides the extra grip that your hands don't have. (I've heard that putting on a pair of rubber cleaning gloves helps in this respect, too.)
- Reshape the bristles on an old broom. When any of my brooms' bristles started going every which way but down, I used to think it was time to buy a new broom. But then I learned this trick: put a rubber band around the bottom of the bristles and let it sit for a few days. When you take the rubber band off again, voila, you've got newly tamed bristles, and a perfectly good broom once again.

Total Savings in This Chapter

The whole idea behind this chapter is to avoid having to spend money on things you would normally buy or pay for. So my deciding to swap books rather than buy new as I did in my prefrugal life would add up to at least $800 in savings each year. In addition, choosing to barter for goods and services secured me $400 in hair-styling services in one year without my spending a dime.

Possible savings in Chapter 11: $1,200 a year

chapter twelve

HOLIDAYS, CELEBRATIONS, AND ENTERTAINING

When it comes to celebrating special events or entertaining guests for the holidays, it's so easy to forget about your budget. You probably want to go all out and throw caution (and coupons) to the wind. But now that you're devoted to living frugally, you can't be a miser for eleven months of the year and then a spendthrift for that remaining month. It's like eating healthy all week long, only to binge on the weekends.

In this chapter I'll help you put your holiday, celebration, and entertaining spending on a diet. I'll guide you through ways to celebrate on the cheap, and shower your friends and loved ones with gifts that don't go over the top financially. Plus I'll give you tips on how you can plan ahead for gift purchases and save money in the future.

Birthdays

If you have kids, you've probably noticed the recent trend of "outsourcing" kids' birthday parties. I've lost count of how many birthdays I've been to at places such as Chuck E. Cheese, gymnastic schools, and other locations where all you have to do is show up for the party—the employees at the place do all of the work for you.

I'll admit that I've outsourced my daughters' birthday parties. But once we started pinching our pennies, we tried our hardest to simplify the birthday celebrations. It helps that when we moved, we bought a house with a swimming pool. Since both of my daughters have summer birthdays, it was natural for them to have a pool party, and that's what we've done for the past few years. It really has simplified the whole birthday experience by not having to go somewhere else for the party. Though a birthday at home isn't free, it's a lot cheaper than one where you've got to pay a per-head fee.

This past year, my youngest daughter really got into this idea of having a frugal birthday. I'm sure part of the incentive was the fact that I was making her pay for part of the party—I mean, my kids hoard their money. (I swear they often have more cash in their wallets than their dad and I do!) She also decided the party should be as green as possible, and if you know anything about green and frugal, you know they often go hand in hand.

My daughter wanted her party to have a backyard barbecue theme, so she worked around that idea as she planned the party's details. Here are some of the things she did, which you might consider as you think frugally when planning a kids' birthday:

- Used Evite.com to invite her friends. While definitely cheaper and more eco-friendly than buying invitations, I've since learned that not all kids check their e-mail as often as you would like—especially if you're sending an invitation with an RSVP date. In the future I might follow up an Evite invitation with a paper invitation made on the computer for free, or I'll make sure that the Evite goes to their parents' e-mail addresses as well.

- Bought reusable red-and-white checked tablecloths. Sure, we'd set them out for her party, but afterward, we could clean them off, fold them up, and use them again at a future event.
- Invested in reusable plastic cups for serving drinks and for using for favors. My daughter bought twice as many cups as she would need for the party. She filled half of the cups with candy to give out to her friends, and then we put the other half out for drinks with the meal. The cups that stayed behind have become a staple for when we eat dinner outside on the patio.
- Cooked the food at home. This included all the trappings of a barbecue, such as hot dogs.
- Baked the cake ourselves. By stocking up on boxed cake mix and frosting when they were on sale for about a buck a package at the supermarket, I was able to whip up a double-layer cake for her party for less than $4. A similar cake at the grocery store would have set us back at least $30. Plus, this way my daughter was in full control of the flavor of the cake and frosting, and how it was decorated.

Weddings and Other Celebrations

When I was spending most of my professional time writing wedding-planning books, I was constantly amazed by how much the average American couple spent on a wedding. In many instances this one-day event would cost more than a year's starting salary—or at least a starting salary in publishing, the industry I know best. In a note of shameless self-promotion, I have to mention that one of the thirteen books I'd written before this one was a book on planning a frugal wedding: *Tie the Knot on a Shoestring.* That book focused on planning a wedding for about $5,000—amazing when you consider that the average American wedding costs about $30,000. Who wouldn't want to learn how to save $25,000 on a wedding?

But I'm not here to sell you on buying my other books; I'm here to offer tips on planning a frugal wedding. With that in mind, here are nine ways you can pull off a wedding (or bat mitzvah or anniversary party) on the cheap without looking like a cheapskate:

1. Think local and in season when planning your menu and any decorations. If your food and flowers don't have to travel a great distance to get to your party, you won't pay a premium to get them.
2. If there is a warehouse club such as Costco nearby, consider getting your wedding cake there. Sure, it will just be a sheet cake versus a tower cake, but you'll get a sugar rush just from the money you would save. Trust me on this!
3. Don't be shy about using swap services or thrift stores to get supplies for your celebration. It's not unreasonable to expect to find decorations such as ribbons, tablecloths, and containers for centerpieces, or even wedding attire, via Freecycle, Goodwill, or your local thrift store. Even garage and yard sales might prove to be a treasure trove of supplies.

❹ Invite people virtually or at least inexpensively. As with birthday invitations, you can save a ton on your wedding invitations by sending them out via Evite (*www.evite.com*) or Pingg (*www.pingg.com*). If you've got older people in your family who might not be on e-mail, you can go for traditional invitations, but through a company or store that can make them for you inexpensively. I'm thinking specifically of Vista Print (*www.vistaprint.com*—I use them for my business cards and stationery) or Party City (*www.partycity.com*). You could also design and print your own invitations and programs using specialty papers you can get at office supply stores. Here's another great way to save money on your invitation kits—use a postcard for RSVPs (saves on paper and postage), and post directions online.

❺ Think carefully about time of the year, day of the week, and time of the day when planning your special occasion—especially an event that uses a catering hall or event space. Saturdays in June, July, September, and October are the most expensive times to plan something such as a wedding. That's prime time in that industry, and you'll pay handsomely to say "I do" then. Move your event to Friday or Sunday, and you might save a bit. Change the month and you'll save more. Pick a day when hardly anyone is interested in going to a party—say, Super Bowl Sunday—and you could save a bundle!

❻ DIY your decorations and accessories. In Chapter 8, "Becoming a Do-It-Yourselfer," I talked about learning to do things for yourself to save money, and part of that advice included learning to become crafty. This suggestion applies to a wedding or other kind of celebration where you might need or want handmade accessories (such as a veil) or centerpieces. If you signed up for a class at Jo-Ann Fabrics and Crafts (*www.joann.com*), for instance, you can learn to make items for your wedding. Plus, if you invited your girlfriends, you could do a combination girls' day out and craft-making session.

7. Skip the favors altogether. I once did a story for a bridal magazine in which I suggested making a donation to charity in lieu of giving out tacky favors. This is appropriate advice for a frugal book, too. In researching that story, I discovered that couples who made decent donations to a charity ended up spending less overall than if they'd purchased traditional favors. So you end up with money in the bank and the comfort of knowing that you helped a good cause, too. For more information on charitable donations to commemorate a special event, visit *www.idofoundation.org*.
8. Tap into the talent you know to help you save money on your special event. A friend who bakes might make your cake for you, and an amateur shutterbug could take care of the wedding pictures as her gift to you. Even if you don't know pros whom you can hire for your wedding or other special occasion, maybe friends or neighbors do. And if they refer you, perhaps you can negotiate for a "friends and family" discount. Hey, it never hurts to ask!
9. Spin your own tunes! These days, deejays are setting up shop at events with their iPods fired up and ready to go. Why pay the middleman for music when you can put together a party playlist on your own iPod or MP3 player? This option makes a lot of sense if you're willing to forgo the kitschy commentary of a deejay or bandleader.

Everything Gifts

As with so many other areas of frugal living, you'll save the most money on things such as gifts if you plan ahead. This is why I like to shop for presents for my friends and family all year long—not just in the weeks leading up to the holidays or their birthday. If I see something in May that I think my mother would like for Christmas—and the price is too good to pass up—I'll buy that item. There's no reason for me, or for you, to pay top prices for a gift when, with a bit of planning, you could get it at a significant savings earlier in the year.

Buying early is also a good idea because when you're in a rush, you usually end up grabbing something without giving it much thought, and spending more than you'd anticipated. That's why I created my gift closet to avoid this kind of frenzied buying.

SEAL OF APPROVAL *GIFT CLOSET*

A few years ago I got the idea to start a gift closet—a place where I could stash gift supplies so that I always had hostess gifts, kids' birthday presents, or other all-occasion gifts on hand.

Some of my favorite items to keep in a gift closet include bags of whole-bean coffee, savory bottles of olive oil, picture frames, note cards, and decorative bowls. Naturally, these are my go-to hostess or teacher gift choices. For kids I'll stock up on games, puzzles, and anything having to do with arts and crafts when I see them on sale at a "too good to pass up" price at the store. Around the holidays, my gift closet expands to my refrigerator, when I add bottles of wine and boxes of chocolate.

Having a gift closet has allowed me to avoid last-minute panicked trips to the store where I'm likely to spend more than I have to on a gift. That's why I recommend that everyone have a gift closet in their home and why I'm giving the notion of a gift closet my Suddenly Frugal Seal of Approval.

It's Okay to Regift

Think I'm crazy to suggest you consider regifting? Well, consider this. Recently, eBay did a survey on regifting, and discovered that the following were the most popular items to regift:

- Wine, champagne, or spirits (21%)
- Trinkets or collectibles (21%)
- Beauty or bath products (21%)
- DVDs, CDs, or books (16%)
- Electronics/appliances (14%)
- Fruitcake (14%)

Okay, so I might draw the line at a fruitcake. However, it just goes to show you that if you receive any nonperishable food and want to pass it along to someone else, you're not going to be the only one doing so.

Starting a Gift Closet

If you've never considered starting a gift closet, here are three tips for getting one going.

1. Find a spot in your house where you have enough room to keep these last-minute gifts and where you won't lose

them. Don't just toss them in a bin you keep under the stairs. Dedicate a shelf in your pantry or even a drawer in a dresser to your gift-closet stash.

2. Stock up throughout the year when you find items on clearance. So at the end of the summer, you can get kids' presents for water fun, such as beach towels, goggles, or inflatable pool toys. In September, when school supplies get marked down, grab crayons, markers, and notepads on clearance for future birthday presents. The day after Christmas? Stock up on Christmas ornaments, scented candles, or even festive cocktail napkins—all appropriate hostess gifts that you can bring with you to holiday parties next year.
3. Put gifts you've received but don't like or can't return in your gift closet. Yes, I am recommending that you use your gift closet as a place for future regifting. Why not? I don't think there's anything wrong with regifting, especially if you happen to have received what I call an all-occasion gift. I describe these as items that are ready-made for regifting. These include picture frames, note cards, candles, soaps, and more. These are the kinds of items that I normally keep in my gift closet and that all make perfect last-minute hostess gifts.

Holidays and Entertaining

When it comes to the holidays, if you're not spending money on gifts, then you're probably bleeding cash stocking up on food or turning your ho-hum house into something festively decorated. But if you've taken my advice above for holiday shopping all year round, or at least have been stocking your gift closet, then hopefully come next holiday season you won't go over budget on your gift spending. Now I'd like to focus on the care and feeding of holiday decorations and any guests you may be hosting this year, and how you can do all of that by spending as little as possible.

Holiday Decorations

Last year I managed to spend pretty much zero on holiday decorations. That's not too bad considering the average American spends about $75 on decorations each holiday season. I was even featured in a *Philadelphia Inquirer* story that shared my tips for making my house festive without returning to my spendthrift ways, such as how I:

- Stacked clementines in a hurricane jar and used it as a centerpiece. (My daughter ate the clementines when the holidays were over.)
- Collected pinecones from a nearby park, and clustered them in glass bowls throughout the house as a decoration. I also put leftover Christmas ornaments in bowls.
- Reused a grapevine wreath that was a centerpiece at my wedding by hanging it on the front door instead of buying a new evergreen wreath that I'd just end up tossing in the compost pile when it turned brown.
- Cut evergreen boughs from my backyard for decorating my fireplace mantel.
- Turned obsolete computer CDs into shiny tree ornaments, or used them as coasters.

See if any of these ideas might work for you—or inspire you to find creative ways to reuse everyday items—as you take a frugal approach to decorating your house this holiday season.

Entertaining

There are a number of ways that you can feed family, friends, and guests at the holidays (or other kinds of celebrations) without breaking your budget. The best part is that they won't even know that you're serving them a frugal menu. Here are seven tips to help you in that respect.

1. Start planning your menu weeks ahead of time. This will give you the chance to stock up on foods when they are on sale (especially those that freeze well or don't need refrigeration), or when you have a coupon for them. For example, your supermarket is going to be promoting cans of pumpkin-pie filling and bags of marshmallows in the weeks before Thanksgiving, but you may just discover that these items are actually cheaper in August or September. And if you happen to find a coupon for them? Score! Some experts I've spoken to say that you can save as much as $75 on a holiday meal just by stocking up when things are on sale.
2. If you know you'll be using fruits and vegetables that you can buy fresh, canned, or frozen, go with the frozen variety. Not only will frozen produce last longer (for an obvious, very cold reason), but frozen fruits and vegetables are actually cheaper in the long run than their canned variety. Though the unit price may show the canned version as the better buy, when you buy something in a can, you're paying for the weight of the metal and the water inside. With frozen fruit and vegetables, there is neither the heavy packaging nor the water to add to its weight.
3. If you're cooking any cuts of meats that you want to marinate, don't waste your money on fancy marinades. You can effectively marinate any meat using two items that you probably already have in your pantry—olive oil and kosher

salt. Use a pastry brush to coat both sides of the meat with the olive oil, then use your fingers to rub in the salt, also on both sides. These two items will give you as tasty a piece of meat as that commercially marketed marinade, without the extra expense. By the same token, save yourself some dough on salad dressings, and simply serve olive oil and balsamic vinegar.

4. Befriend the butcher at your local market. The butcher can let you know when your favorite cut of meat is going to go on sale so you'll know to stock up when that sale does come along. Also, don't be afraid to ask the butcher to cut up on-sale meat into smaller portions so you can serve some at the holidays, and then freeze the rest for meals in the future. We did that last year when we discovered pork loin on sale for a crazy cheap price. We had the butcher give us four one-pound cuts of pork loin, two of which we served at dinner. With the other two we used our Food Saver (*www.foodsaver.com*) to vacuum seal the packages, and then we stored them in the freezer for dinner at a later date.
5. Crunch some numbers before you decide to do your own catering. Let's say that you want to serve a fresh fruit salad or fruit plate at a celebration. Depending on what time of the year it is and whether or not the fruits you want to serve are in season, it might actually be more expensive for you to make that fruit salad or fruit plate yourself, if you have to buy each piece of fruit and cut it up. This is where a warehouse club can come in handy. You can buy a prepared fruit plate the size you need for your party, and you might just spend less in the end.
6. Practice portion control to get more bang for your food buck. This isn't about putting your guests on a diet. But if you can have some control over the portion sizes of the

food you're serving, you can make a little bit of food last longer. So in addition to putting out smaller plates—people pile less food on smaller plates and may not come back for seconds—precut your meats and desserts, and cook smaller dinner rolls to encourage people to eat less food in one setting. Don't worry—you won't look like a cheapskate if you try this trick. I guarantee your table will still seem to be overflowing with delicious food.

7. Speaking of plates, never take the easy way out and go for disposable plates, cups, and flatware. For obvious reasons this doesn't make any frugal sense. If you're freaking out that you won't have enough place settings to accommodate all of your guests, borrow from family, friends, and neighbors. Mismatched dishes can add a certain *je ne sais quoi* to a festive gathering. Okay, well at least they'll be a conversation starter! In addition, it goes without saying that you should be setting your table with cloth napkins. Yes, using fabric napkins gives you some laundry to do but in the long run you'll save money by not buying disposable napkins.

Freezing the Smart Way

When you freeze cuts of meat, be sure to write the date right on the package when you put the package in the freezer. (Sharpie markers work wonderfully in this respect.) Food experts advise not freezing meat for longer than six months. By having the date right there where you can see it, you can feel confident that you'll remember to cook the meat before it goes bad, and therefore you won't have ended up wasting money on your great deal.

Total Savings in This Chapter

I hope this chapter showed you how easy it is to put together small savings here and there through the holiday and entertaining season. From stocking a gift closet to avoiding last-minute, in-a-panic trips to the store to get a hostess gift to stocking up on boxed cake mix when it's on sale at the supermarket so you can avoid paying a big-time retail price for a birthday cake, these are all tips that add up over time.

Possible savings in Chapter 12: $180 a year on entertaining and a whopping $25,000 on a wedding!

chapter thirteen

DON'T THROW IT OUT— WEAR IT OUT

There is an old New England adage that goes like this: Use it up, wear it out. Make it do, or do without. Or, as Tim "Project Runway" Gunn says, "Make it work." What does all that have to do with the new frugality? Tons. This chapter shows you how to give new life to old stuff. And even if you can't use something again, it will tell you how your old possessions can benefit others.

You probably live in a community that offers recycling services. And if you're like me, when you're done with something that is recyclable, you just toss it in the recycling bin and don't give it another thought. But did you ever stop to think about how you might be able to reuse those recyclables in a way that would save you money? In this chapter, I've outlined some of the most common kinds of items that you're likely already recycling but could be repurposing for a second life. With a little bit of reusing effort, you're going to save yourself a lot of money.

Office Paper

Even if you don't have a home office, chances are you've got piles and piles of office paper moving through your house on a regular basis. Probably on any given day you're putting everything from school permission slips to magazine subscription cards into the recycling bin.

When you get those permission slips or memos from work, check to see if they're printed on both sides. If they're not, tear the sheets in half, then staple a pile together. Guess what you've got? A free notepad for writing down phone messages or shopping lists, or scratch paper that your kids can use when they need to do some computing for their homework.

One of my daughter's teachers got her colleagues to save old worksheets that they normally would have recycled, and then had the industrial arts teacher bind them into notepads. I don't mind if a note from the teacher comes home with something unrelated printed on the back—I know that the teacher is reusing the paper, which saves the school district, and the taxpayers, money.

Finally, if you tend to ship lots of things or need to store breakables, you could always put your office paper in the shredder and then use the shredded paper in lieu of purchasing packing peanuts or bubble wrap. I know people who also reuse shredded paper as cat litter in a pinch or to line a hamster cage.

As far as Mother Nature is concerned, we've kept a lot of paper out of the recycling stream for longer, and we've saved money, too. That's why I'm giving printing on both sides of the paper my Suddenly Frugal Seal of Approval.

SEAL OF APPROVAL *PRINTING ON BOTH SIDES OF THE PAPER*

A great way to save money in your home office is to print out documents, maps, and your kids' homework on the blank side of a used piece of paper. In my house, you're not allowed to place a piece of paper in the recycling bin until you've used both sides of it.

Before we instilled this printing-on-both-sides-of-the-paper rule, we would go through a case of office paper every six months. That added up to 5,000 sheets of paper we were using up and wasting every six months. Then when I started getting everyone to print on both sides of the paper, I found that we could go almost a year between buying cases of it. That change alone saved us $50.

Envelopes

How many times a week do you get something in the mail that comes with a blank envelope—either one with a window or an address already printed on it? I know that I get them at least once a day . . . which means that I end up with a lot of envelopes that end up in the recycling bin. While it's true that you can't reuse the envelopes as-is to mail stuff if they already have a bar code printed on the bottom, but put a plain white mailing label or sticker on to block out the bar code, and you've got yourself a free envelope.

Instead of spending money on envelopes at an office supply store, why not stock up on these kinds of envelopes? In addition to using them for sending something via the United States Postal Service, you can keep them around for sending back permission slips to school or for holding coupons when you go shopping.

Reusing Envelopes to Hold Coupons

Here's how I use envelopes to help me stay organized when I grocery shop. First, I find two envelopes from my stash—one large envelope and one that's smaller and fits inside the larger one. I put the smaller envelope inside the larger one. I take the shopping list that I've got tacked up on the refrigerator, and then I secure it to the back of the bigger envelope, using tape, glue, or staples. Then I go through my coupons to see which of them match up with what I'm going to buy at the store that day. I place those coupons in front of the smaller envelope, inside the bigger envelope, and head out to the store.

Once I start shopping, I do one of two things with the coupons.

1. If I'm going to use a coupon when I check out, I put it inside the smaller envelope.
2. If I'm not going to use it, I move it behind the smaller envelope.

This way, I don't have to fumble for the coupons when it's time to pay. I simply take the smaller envelope out of the bigger one.

Newspaper

There are three quick ways you can reuse newspapers to save you money:

1. If you have a fireplace, you can stockpile them to use as your fire starters.

2. You can crumple them and use them as packing material if you're moving, storing, or sending something in a box.
3. You can take the Sunday comics and, like your mom might have done, use it as in-a-pinch wrapping paper to cover a gift.

Cereal Boxes

Before I give you some ways to reuse cereal boxes—and save yourself some dough—let me ask you this: did you know that the waxy bag inside the cereal box is actually recyclable? These cereal bags are considered to be #2 plastic or HDPE. That stands for high-density polyethylene, but you probably know it best as the plastic that milk jugs are made of. If your curbside recycling program accepts #2 plastic—which nearly all do—then you can toss the cereal box liner in with the used-up milk jugs and laundry-detergent bottles.

Okay, so now what to do with cereal boxes instead of just flattening them and recycling them? Here are two ideas:

- Use them as gift boxes. Clearly, you'll want to shake out any residual crumbs left from breakfast cereal, and maybe give the inside of the box a quick wipe with a slightly moist rag. But once that's done, a cereal box makes a perfectly good gift box. If you think about it, the average-sized cereal box (based on what I have in my cabinet right now) is 11" × 7½" × 2". That's about the same size as a gift box you might get in a store. Just slide the present inside, fold down the flaps and wrap as you would any other present.
- Turn them into magazine holders. I'm a huge fan of those standup magazine holders. You know the ones I'm talking

about—they sit on a shelf, with one side partially "cut out" so you can store your magazines all together, spine facing out. You can buy gorgeous ones at most retail stores for between $5 and $20, but why spend money when you can easily make one?

For this idea, use one of the biggest cereal boxes you can find, such as a twenty-five-ounce box of Cheerios. Along with the empty cereal box you'll need a razor knife, and, if you want, paper to cover the box with or spray paint for painting the box. Here are five steps to transform a cereal box into a magazine holder:

1. With your razor knife, start at the upper corner of the front of the cereal box (it's the wide side of the box) and slice, on a diagonal, about three-quarters of the way down the box.
2. Reposition the razor knife to cut from the end of the diagonal line you just cut, and take it out in a horizontal line to the side of the box.
3. Flip the box around so that the back side is facing you now. Follow steps 1 and 2 again. Note: make sure you're slicing from the same upper corner as on the front of the box.
4. Discard the cut-out pieces of the cereal box (in the recycling bin, please, not the trash), and, voilà, you've got the basic shape of a magazine holder.
5. (Optional) If you'd rather not have a reused box of cereal on display in your home office or wherever it is that you store your magazines, you can spray-paint or cover the box. Use wrapping paper, tacky shelf paper, or any wallpaper you might have left over from a home-improvement project.

At any given time, I have between eight and ten of these kinds of magazine holders in my office. By making these holders myself, I can save as much as $200. And if the cardboard starts to age and give way, I can simply make myself a new one!

Cardboard Toilet Paper and Paper Towel Rolls

If you've read my Suddenly Frugal blog in the past, then you know I've talked a few times about ways to reuse toilet paper rolls and paper towel rolls. Some people are completely skeeved out by the notion of reusing a toilet paper roll, since they assume it's all germy from being in a bathroom. Fine; those germophobes can just recycle them with their other cardboard. But for the rest of us looking for reuses? Here are some suggestions you may not have considered.

Cord Control

You can buy these fancy cord contraptions in the store that funnel all of your electrical cords in a single line so that you don't have tangles under your desk. But they cost money—anywhere from $5 to $55. Well, a cardboard paper towel tube can do the same and for free. True, the cardboard version isn't as pretty but at least it's free and functional. You can always take the time to spray-paint the tubes, as you might a cereal box you've turned into a magazine holder, so they won't be so ugly.

Seed Starters

Cardboard tubes make excellent seed starters—perfect for the gardener who is trapped inside all winter. They're really easy to make, too. All you need to do is cut a toilet paper tube in half (to make two short tubes) with a pair of scissors, and then fold in the edges of one end of each tube to make a bottom. Next, fill both tubes with soil and your seeds, and you're ready to grow something in the two planters you've just made.

Note: you can reuse opaque milk cartons, cut in half, and/or plastic yogurt cups in a similar fashion for starting a plant. But what makes a toilet paper roll seed starter even better is that you can plant it right in your garden once the ground thaws. Cardboard is biodegradable, so the toilet paper roll will disintegrate over time as the plant grows.

Holiday Decorations and Storage

Both toilet paper and paper towel rolls are really handy around the holidays—before, during, and after.

- You could string a bunch of toilet paper tubes together into a wreath shape, then spray-paint it green for a green-and-frugal Christmas wreath.
- You could use them to make homemade Christmas "crackers." These crackers aren't food but rather a festive tradition from the U.K. Christmas crackers are wrapped cylinders that include a prize. Here's how you make one: fill the cardboard tube with candy or even money from your change jar, wrap the tube with wrapping paper, and then pinch the ends and tie them with ribbon. Kids will love opening them at the holidays.
- You can also reuse cardboard paper towel tubes to store your decorations. You can string lights around them so you'll avoid having them become a tangled mess. Do you have individual candles that you place in your windows to give your home a festive feel after dark or on the dinner table when you're

entertaining? You can slip each candle inside a paper towel roll to prevent it from breaking when you put it away.

Plastic Bag Storage

It's hard to believe, but once, many years ago, we spent money on a contraption to hold our plastic bags. It had a honeycomb design that looked pretty, but the bags were always getting snagged on the edges of the honeycomb whenever we tried to pull a bag out, so it ended up being a waste of money. I don't want you to make the same mistake, and that's why I'm suggesting that you reuse a paper towel roll as an easy, free storage container for plastic bags.

All you have to do is cover one end of the tube with your hand and then stuff as many bags as you can fit into the tube. The bags get compressed together and don't fall out. (If you're concerned that the bags will fall out, pinch in one end, like the seed starters mentioned previously.) Then, when you need bags, you can pull them out, one by one, as you do tissues from a box. Not only is this mini storage device great in the kitchen but it can come in handy in the car, too. Just slip it into the glove compartment or even the trunk. Then you'll never be without a go-to garbage bag whenever you decide to clean out the car or take the dog for an impromptu walk.

Rodent Playground

Who needs to spend money on plastic Habitrails or other kinds of commercial pet toys when you could toss in a paper towel or toilet paper roll with your gerbil, hamster, or mouse? I've heard from people who keep these kinds of pets that not only do these little guys love to play inside the tubes—hide and seek, anyone?—but they also like chewing them to bits.

How Brown Paper Bags Become Free Book Covers

Raise your hand if you ever made a textbook cover out of a brown paper bag that you got at the supermarket. That's still a great use for a brown paper grocery bag. While stretchy book covers are all the rage these days with school kids, you don't have to spend money on them if you've got brown paper bags lying around. Making a book cover is so easy. Here are the seven steps to make one:

1. Cut the paper bag open and remove the flap that was the bottom of the bag. This will leave you with a big piece of brown paper.
2. Place the paper horizontally on a flat surface and center the closed book on it.
3. Fold the paper in on the left and the right so that it fits snugly around the front cover and back cover of the book. Crease where you've just folded the paper and let the "flap" flop back.
4. Use a pencil to outline where the top and the bottom of the textbook sit on the paper. Remove the book.
5. Fold down the top and bottom "flaps" so the paper is the same height as the textbook.
6. Fold in the side flaps at the creases.
7. You'll now have a "sleeve" on both the right and the left into which you can slip the front cover and the back cover of the book.

Glass Jars

From the looks of my husband's workroom, you would think that we're still having babies. That's because he's got shelf after shelf lined with baby food jars, all of which hold various home improvement tools. From screws to nails to washers, my husband has figured out a way to store everything in plain sight in these little glass jars. Not only is he smart in keeping himself organized this way, but he's also being quite frugal. Jars of all sizes make great storage containers, whether you use them in your workroom, shed, craft room, kitchen, or basement. Here are just a few ideas:

- You can use washed-out jars to hold dry pasta, loose change, or even premeasured servings of cereal.
- A glass jar could also pass for a makeshift vase.
- If you're doing DIY holiday presents this year, you can reuse a jar to contain whatever food goodie you're giving out. For example, you could fill the jar with the dry ingredients of a chocolate chip cookie mix, and then attach a tag to the top with instructions on making your secret recipe (assuming you have a secret recipe).

Unfortunately, a lot of manufacturers have switched from using glass jars to plastic jars, which don't clean up as nicely as glass. Plastic jars also aren't as easily repurposed. I find that often the plastic retains the smell of its original occupant. Plus, a plastic jar simply isn't as pretty as a jar that once held tomato sauce and now doubles as a mason jar. But that doesn't mean the glass jars aren't out there. I'm still buying salsa, tomato sauce, and jelly in glass jars that I could easily repurpose once they are empty and washed.

Worn-Out Place Mats

When we moved into this house a few years ago, the previous owners left a shelf full of cleaning supplies and random objects, including rolls of that sticky Swiss cheese–like liner that you use in drawers. Slowly, I've been going through those liners as I clean out, organize, and reline the drawers in my kitchen. Recently, though, I ran out, so half of my drawers had liner in them and the other half didn't. There was no way I could end my day with my kitchen drawers in an upheaval. I started frantically searching for any additional rolls of drawer liner—under the stairs, in the basement, in the hall closet—but no luck. What was I going to do?

Then I realized that in my linen drawer, I had more fabric place mats than I knew what to do with. Many of them had seen better days, but I just hadn't gotten around to getting rid of them because I knew—just knew—that I might be able to repurpose them one day. Well, that was the day. I discovered that place mats can be the perfect stand-in for a drawer liner. Many of my kitchen drawers are somewhat narrow, and when I slid the place mats into them, they bent up around the edges. This was fine with me, because it added a layer on the sides of the drawers that prevented the contents (silverware, wooden spoons, and the like) from sliding around or, worse, sliding under the place mat/drawer liner where they might be lost forever.

Here's the best part about using fabric place mats as drawer liners: should they get dirty—and I'm sure they will—I can just take them out, wash and dry them, and put them back into the drawer. With the other kind of drawer liner, once they got dirty, I always had to throw them out and replace them with a new sheet of liner. So not only will I be saving myself money by not having to buy new drawer liners, I'll also be cutting down on my trash because I won't be throwing them away anymore.

Total Savings in This Chapter

I love it when being frugal also equals being green. And in a sense that's what this whole chapter has been about. When you repurpose items you already own, you save yourself money, and you help to save Mother Earth by not adding to the landfills.

All told, in this chapter I helped you to uncover how to save money in simple ways, such as repurposing cereal boxes into magazine holders, reusing paper by printing on both sides, and turning used paper towel rolls into cord organizers.

Possible savings in Chapter 13: >$300 a year

chapter fourteen

VACATIONS AND GETAWAYS

Even frugal people get to take vacations. They just might not take the same kinds of vacations as the spendthrifts among us. I love that one of the hottest trends these days is something called the "staycation," where you stay close to home (if not at home) during your vacation. This chapter will tell you how to make the most of your time off—even if you decide you want to vacation right at home.

Vacations on the Cheap

The best way to save money on a vacation is to take advantage of free or low-cost resources that can help you spend as little as possible during your time off. Those resources could be a friend's guest room, which allows you to get lodging for free, or maybe a timeshare-swapping service.

You can make timeshares work for you in two ways:

1. If you actually own a timeshare, you likely have a membership through a company such as RCI (*www.rci.com*) or Interval (*www.intervalworld.com*). These companies manage your timeshare weeks and allow you to trade them for vacations elsewhere around the country, often at significantly reduced prices. We once did a timeshare exchange for a resort in Walt Disney World that turned out to be a fully stocked condominium, with three bedrooms, two baths, and a full kitchen, and it cost us $150 to stay for the week. A comparable stay at a hotel may have cost us $150 per night—or $1,050 for the week.
2. If you know someone who owns a timeshare, you might be able to borrow or rent it for your vacation. We've done this with friends and family in the past.

But if you don't own a timeshare, have no desire to buy one, or don't know anyone who has one, there are other ways for you to plan a frugal vacation—whether it's in your hometown, in the next state, or clear across the country.

Entertainment Book

If you live in or are planning to travel to one of the 150 "markets" in the United States, Canada, or Puerto Rico that the Entertainment Books cover, then investing in one of these discount books would be money well spent. In case you're not familiar with them, the Entertainment Books (*www.entertainment.com*) are directories to local businesses and services that include money-off coupons to nearby businesses. Each book contains thousands of ways to save on the things you do every day, such as buy-one-get-one free deals at local restaurants, free admission coupons to the zoo, and sports and entertainment venues—all things that you could conceivably do on vacation as well. In addition, if you register on the Entertainment Book website, you'll receive additional coupon offers via e-mail on a weekly basis.

While the books cost between $25 and $40 (depending on the market), the average Entertainment Book user saves $175 from taking advantage of the offers in the book. Excluding your initial investment, that means that this book can help you save at least $100 on a vacation. Note: if you do invest in an Entertainment Book, keep it in your car with you at all times. That way, you'll always have the Entertainment Book at the ready so you can scan it for coupons. It really won't help you save money when it's sitting in your hotel room or back home on your coffee table.

Cities on the Cheap

A freelance writer friend of mine named Jennifer Maciejewski started the Cities on the Cheap (*www.citiesonthecheap.com*) concept in late 2008, when the country was just starting to sink into a recession. Maciejewski, based in Atlanta, originated the idea with Atlanta on the Cheap as a way for her to uncover free or low-cost options for family entertainment that she could use with her own family. Quickly the "on the cheap" idea caught on, and early in 2009 she rolled it out nationwide.

You can visit an "on the cheap" city blog at any time and find out about free dance performances, concerts, art workshops, coffee, breakfast, poetry slams, and movie passes. That's in addition to dozens of deals on everything from Broadway shows to sporting events. Currently, there are more than forty city "on the cheap" blogs in the U.S. and Canada, from Arizona to New York, with more in development.

In addition to city-specific sites, one specialty site, Disney on the Cheap, focuses on deals for visiting the Florida theme parks, and the other, Florida on the Cheap, focuses on Florida's tourist attractions.

Association Memberships

When you joined an association or renewed your membership, have you gotten discount cards for travel-related services with your membership card? And have you ever put those discounts to good use? If not, the next time you're planning a trip, see if any of the membership codes on those cards can get you a better rate on a hotel stay or a rental car.

Travel Discounts Through AAA

Many people think of AAA (Automobile Association of America) membership as something they need for roadside assistance with their car. But being an AAA member can provide financial benefits when you're planning a vacation. My AAA membership has saved me a ton of money on hotel rooms, even when a call to the hotel resulted in them telling me that no discounted rooms were available for my stay. However, when I showed up at the front desk of the hotel and presented my AAA card, many times I could get a discounted room on the spot. An AAA card can secure all kinds of travel-related discounts, from money off amusement park and museum admission fees to deals at local restaurants. Visit *www.aaa.com* for more information. Note: the website will prompt you to enter your zip code, which will then bring you to one of the sixty-nine local AAA clubs nationwide.

Other organizations, associations, and memberships that provide discount travel cards might include:

- College and university alumni groups
- Professional associations (my memberships in two writing organizations—the Authors Guild and the American

Society of Journalists and Authors—both come with travel discount offers)
- Your employer

Credit Cards

I hope that if you use a credit card on a regular basis you're earning some sort of "reward" for being a customer. For example, I earn points toward free groceries or gift cards to home-improvement stores when I use a certain MasterCard. Many credit cards offer points toward hotel affinity programs, which are often easier to cash in than frequent-flier miles. Some of these programs have changed due to recent changes in the credit industry, so read the fine print carefully. Check to see if some of the rewards that your credit card offers could help you, in one way or another, enjoy a frugal vacation the next time you want to get away.

Staycations

Perhaps the biggest "travel" trend to come out of this economic downturn is the notion of "staycations," when people stay home for their vacation. Before it had this clever name, lots of people were already taking vacations locally, encouraged by such things as, for example, my county's annual summer promotion of "act like a tourist in your own town." What a fun idea—figuring out how to find vacation-like activities within your own area code. And if you're looking to sneak in a minivacation without spending big bucks, this is an idea with legs. Here are five ways you can plan a staycation for your next vacation.

❶ Find a nearby amusement park or water park. Are there amusement and water parks close to your home that you haven't had the time to get to or just never bothered checking out because they're right in your backyard? Obviously those who live in the Orlando area are well aware of their Disney, Universal Studios, and SeaWorld neighbors. But what about the rest of us? Many amusement parks will offer discounted season passes to people who live nearby. Also, if you buy the Entertainment Book (mentioned on page 218), you might be able to score an admission discount.

❷ Take yourself (and your family) to a minor league baseball game. Sure, I've got a major league baseball team whose games I could go to (though it's a bit of a haul and a lot of cha-ching for tickets), but within a forty-five-minute radius of my home I've got a better, closer, and more affordable option: three minor league baseball teams and a professional softball team. Our family of four can have a wonderful night out for under $50!

❸ Explore local museums. I make it a point to visit major museums when I visit big cities (Philadelphia Museum of Art when I'm in Philly, Metropolitan Museum of Art when I'm in the Big Apple), but I often forget that there are a number of terrific (albeit smaller) museums that are a short drive away. On a hot summer day, what could be more refreshing than spending a day inside with air conditioning and appreciating local art? Also, it's often cheaper to join a museum as a member than to pay admission à la carte. By joining a museum you're supporting a local institution, you've got an economical destination for other day trips in the future, and then when you're invited to openings (which members inevitably are), you'll have something to do at night (granted, without the kids) that's free.

4. Rediscover the joy of picnicking. When was the last time your family had a picnic? When I was a kid, my mother would fry up chicken and pack it and some salads in a cooler, and we would go to the beach to enjoy a sunset picnic dinner on the sand. We would always go with some friends so that the grownups could enjoy grownup time together and the kids could run around doing kid things. Even if you just pack up dinner and eat on a blanket spread on your back lawn, that small change of scenery—exchanging your dining room for the backyard—can create a feeling of being away without your having to travel far or spend a lot of money.
5. Enjoy nature or history at a local park. Within an hour's drive of my home, I could spend the day at any number of state and historic parks. These range from a national seashore park in Sandy Hook, New Jersey, to parks that commemorate the Revolutionary War—including Washington Crossing State Park (in both Pennsylvania and New Jersey) as well as Valley Forge. If we wanted to get our history on as part of our staycation plans, we'd have plenty of options to choose from at these local parks. Might the same be true for where you live? To explore your park options nearby, visit the National Park Service's website at *www.nps.gov* or log on to your state, county, or city's official website, and look for links under "parks and recreations" or something similar.

SEAL OF APPROVAL *SOUTHWEST AIRLINES*

While you may think that the cheapest way for you to travel on vacation is by car, the truth is if you're going somewhere that Southwest Airlines flies, I strongly suggest you check the airline's website (*www.southwest.com*) first before gassing up the car. Southwest runs specials from time to time where you can fly somewhere for about the price of roundtrip train fare. I like Southwest's Business Select fare option, which costs a bit more than the typical inexpensive Southwest fares, but it comes with some extra, worthwhile perks. These include:

- Boarding first.
- Earning extra points in Southwest's frequent-flier program.
- Receiving a free drink coupon when you print out your boarding pass. This is key if you want more than soda during your flight, because Southwest no longer takes cash to pay for drinks. You have to use credit or debit, or you'll be going thirsty. (Soft drinks, coffee, water, and juice are still free.)
- Getting a discount on a car rental.
- Lining up for priority security screening in certain airports that Southwest serves. These include Baltimore Washington International, Dallas, Denver, and Los Angeles.
- Being eligible for a full refund of your fare if you need to cancel or change your flight.

These are some of the reasons why when I travel on business I always try to fly Southwest Airlines and why it has my Suddenly Frugal Seal of Approval.

Total Savings in This Chapter

When it comes to vacations of all kinds, it's easy to spend a lot of money in the blink of an eye—especially if you go to a location where you always feel as if your wallet is open and your money is for the taking. Studies show that the average person spends $1,600 on a summer vacation, but when you're looking to vacation frugally, you just can't lay out that kind of cash. That's why it's a good thing that this chapter uncovered ways that you could save on vacations. These include choosing to have a staycation, using free offers and discount coupons that you can find through services such as the Cities on the Cheap websites and the Entertainment Book, and finding nearby amusement parks that may give locals a discount.

Possible savings in Chapter 14: at least $1,000 on an upcoming vacation

appendix

FOR MORE INFORMATION

Here are website addresses and other information on the blogs, online resources, books, and organizations I've mentioned in the preceding pages.

A Year of Slow Cooking blog: *http://crockpot365.blogspot.com*

American Water Works Association: *www.awwa.org*

Apple Computers Recycling: *www.apple.com/environment*

BankRate.com: *www.bankrate.com*

Bookins.com: *www.bookins.com*

BookMooch.com: *www.bookmooch.com*

Borders Rewards Perks: *www.bordersrewardsperks.com*

Brita filters: *www.brita.com*

Cities on the Cheap Network: *www.citiesonthecheap.com*

Comcast On Demand: *www.comcast.net/tv/on-demand/*

Community Support Agriculture (CSA) farms: *www.localharvest.org*

The Complete Idiot's Guide to Vegetable Gardening by Daria Price Bowman (Alpha Books, 2009)

Consumer Energy Center: *www.consumerenergycenter.org*

Consumer Reports: *www.consumerreports.org*

Cornell University's Co-op Extension: *www.cce.cornell.edu*

Costco: *www.costco.com*

Coupons.com: *www.coupons.com*

Coupon Winner: *www.couponwinner.com*

Coupon Mom: *www.couponmom.com*

Craigslist: *www.craigslist.org*

Crock-Pot: *www.crock-pot.com*

CVS Extra Care Card: *www.cvs.com*

Direct Buy: *www.directbuy.com*

eBay: *www.ebay.com*

Edmunds.com: *www.edumunds.com*

Earth 911: *www.earth911.org*

Energy Star: *www.energystar.gov*

Entertainment Book: *www.entertainment.com*

Environmental Protection Agency: *www.epa.gov*

The Everything® Grow Your Own Vegetables Book by Catherine Abbott (Adams Media, 2010)

Evite: *www.evite.com*

EZ Pass: *www.ezpass.com*

Dryel: *www.dryel.com*

Fabulous & Frugal: *www.fabandfru.com*

Fast Lane: *www.masspike.com*

Food Saver Vacuum Sealing System: *www.foodsaver.com*

Freecycle: *www.freecycle.org*

Freepeats: *www.freepeats.org*

Gap Favorite long-sleeve T-shirts and ribbed undershirts: *www.gap.com*

Goodwill: *www.goodwill.org*

Google Groups: *http://groups.google.com*

Habitat for Humanity ReStore: *www.habitat.org/env/restores.aspx*

Home Depot Clinics: *www.homeimproverclub.com*

Hulu.com: *www.hulu.com*

I-Pass: *www.getipass.com*

I Do Foundation: *www.idofoundation.org*

Interval: *www.intervalworld.com*

Jansport: *www.jansport.com*

Jo-Ann Stores: *www.joann.com*

Kelley Blue Book: *www.kbb.com*

Kitchen shears from Pampered Chef: *www.pamperedchef.com*

Lands' End: *www.landsend.com*

Lauren Fix, The Car Coach: *www.laurenfix.com*

Lennox Industries: *www.lennox.com*

L.L. Bean: *www.llbean.com*

Lowe's: *www.lowes.com*

Make It Fast, Cook It Slow: The Big Book of Everyday Slow Cooking by Stephanie O'Dea (Hyperion, 2009)

Marshalls: *www.marshallsonline.com*

Nalgene bottles: *www.nalgene-outdoor.com*

National Gardening Association: *www.garden.org*

National Park Service: *www.nps.gov*

NeighBORROW: *www.neighborrow.com*

Netflix: *www.netflix.com*

Old Navy: *www.oldnavy.com*

PaperBackSwap.com: *www.paperbackswap.com*

Pampered Chef: *www.pamperedchef.com*

Party City: *www.partycity.com*

Penn State Co-op Extension: *www.extension.psu.edu*

Pingg: *www.pingg.com*

Plato's Closet: *www.platoscloset.com*

Radio Shack's "trade in" program: *www.radioshack.com/tradein*

RCI: *www.rci.com*

Redbox: *www.redbox.com*

RedStickFreeUse: *www.redstickfree.org*

Rubbermaid: *www.rubbermaid.com*

SCORE: *www.score.org*

SheSpeaks: *www.shespeaks.com*

Sodastream soda-making machine: *www.sodaclubusa.com*

Solutions catalog: *www.solutions.com*

Staples Rewards: *www.staples.com*

Starbucks "Grounds for Your Garden": *www.starbucks.com*

Suddenly Frugal (the blog): *www.suddenlyfrugal.com*

Sunpass: *www.sunpass.com*

Swaptree.com: *www.swaptree.com*

Target: *www.target.com*

Tie the Knot on a Shoestring by Leah Ingram (Alpha Books, 2007)

T.J. Maxx: *www.tjmaxx.com*

Trane: *www.trane.com*

Tupperware Sandwich Keeper: *www.tupperware.com*

Twin Cities Free Market: *www.twincitiesfreemarket.org*

United States Forest Service: *www.fs.fed.us*

U.S. Department of Energy's Office of Energy Efficiency and Renewable Energy: *www.eere.energy.gov*

Verizon FiOS TV: *www.verizon.com/fiostv*

VistaPrint: *www.vistaprint.com*

VocalPoint: *www.vocalpoint.com*

Yahoo Groups: *http://groups.yahoo.com*

Ziloks: *http://us.zilok.com/*

Zwaggle.com: *www.zwaggle.com*

INDEX

INDEX

about the author

Leah Ingram is the creator of the nationally syndicated blog called Suddenly Frugal (*www.suddenlyfrugal.com*), and an expert on how families can live more on less. She is also the author of thirteen books, including *Gifts Anytime! How to Find the Perfect Present for Any Occasion* (ASJA Press/iUniverse, 2005), *The Everything® Etiquette Book, 2nd Edition: A Modern-Day Guide to Good Manners* (Adams Media, 2005), and *Tie the Knot on a Shoestring* (Alpha Books, 2007).

In addition, Leah has written hundreds of newspaper, magazine, and website articles on nearly every topic under the sun, including back-to-school savings (*Woman's Day*), planning a wedding that benefits a good cause (*Parade*), and using eBay to shop for prom bargains (*USA Weekend*).

In 2006, a profile she wrote about breast cancer survivors for *Triumph*, an American Cancer Society magazine, received two custom-publishing awards. They were an APEX Award of Excellence for Interviewing and Personal Profiles and a Magnum Opus Silver Medal in Writing.

When she's not writing magazine articles, Leah can be found drinking coffee, walking her dog (often at the same time), and policing her home for lights left on when no one is home.

Leah has appeared on television hundreds of times to discuss family-related topics, including gift tips, etiquette advice, and shopping suggestions. She's been an expert guest on *The CBS Evening News with Katie Couric*, *Good Morning America*, CNBC's *Market Wrap*, *BusinessWeek* TV, *ABC News Now,* and *Good Day New York*, among other programs. In addition, she's acted as a media spokesperson for many national brands, including Bank of America, T-Mobile, and Starbucks.

Leah is a graduate of New York University, with a bachelor of arts in journalism, and the Protocol School of Washington, where she received her certification as an etiquette and protocol consultant. She also trained in TV hosting at TVI Actors Studio in New York City. She lives in New Hope, Pennsylvania, with her husband, two daughters, and faithful canine companion and walking partner, Buff.